Studies in Language and Literature

Emerson R. Marks

Wayne State University

THE POETICS
OF *REASON*

ENGLISH NEOCLASSICAL
CRITICISM

RANDOM HOUSE ≈ NEW YORK

FIRST PRINTING

Copyright © 1968 by Random House, Inc.
All rights reserved under International and Pan-American Copyright Conventions. Published in the United States by Random House, Inc., New York, and simultaneously in Canada by Random House of Canada Limited, Toronto.
Library of Congress Catalog Card Number: 68–17848
Manufactured in the United States of America
by The Colonial Press, Inc., Clinton, Massachusetts
Typography by LEON BOLOGNESE

TO *Herbert M. Schueller*

Foreword

Since it aims at both understanding and evaluation, this study of English neoclassical criticism assumes two dimensions. The first is historical, which means that the literary and critical concepts and practices are always considered in relation to their cultural setting, to neoclassicism in the broadest sense. This of course has been done before and in greater depth than is feasible here. At whatever cost of repetition, however, it must be done again because to shirk it is almost certainly to replace understanding by misconception. If most of the essential points made about the larger intellectual matrix of neoclassical criticism are therefore hardly original, I hope the reader will in compensation find them freshly and independently set forth. The second dimension is nontemporal in the sense that it considers the most characteristic literary theories of the English Enlightenment on their own merits. In effect this is to assess them in the light of subsequent criticism and literary experience. My justification for doing so is the conviction that much of the literary criticism written between the Restoration and the romantic period is of lasting value and deserves to be approached with other than antiquarian interest.

It is easy to speak of viewing and judging *sub specie*

aeternitatis, but in practice this usually means no more than an unconscious application of modern criteria and predilections to the norms and notions of a bygone time. Since every generation constructs its own past, it is always more accurate to speak, for instance, of *our* seventeenth century than of *the* seventeenth century, recognizing that the Victorians, the Romantics, and the Augustans each had theirs. None of them knew or could have known *the* seventeenth century. In this situation there is nothing to apologize for and little to regret. We do have to acknowledge that all human knowing is subject to limitation, but this should only conduce to intellectual humility, which is so far a good thing.

But not too much humility. A current fashion is to conclude that because all knowledge is time-conditioned all knowledge is hopelessly biased. Why, it is asked, should we believe our picture of the Age of Dryden to be any more valid than Matthew Arnold's or George Saintsbury's? This is not the place for a full answer to that question. For the moment it will suffice to reply that we have the considerable advantage (apart from scholarship since accumulated) of knowing something about their John Dryden as well as our own. We can thus assume that each successive age can make an ever closer approximation to a just estimate. If this assumption is illusory it is nonetheless a stimulus to fresh speculation. What matters most is that even if our Dryden is not truer than Arnold's, he is, properly speaking, the only one we can have that will be meaningful to our time and needs.

As a kind of corollary to this approach I would suggest that what we call neoclassicism, and the less apologetic French call *classicisme,* is not simply a phenomenon forever past and irrecoverable. It is also a persistent attitude toward life and art that during the seventeenth and eighteenth centuries found the historical moment favorable to its predominance. In subsequent and more hostile periods this attitude received occasional expression. Its norms and assumptions reappear in the protests against romantic excesses raised in the last century by Sainte-Beuve. His little book on Virgil, whose art was the supreme model of excellence for Augustan men of letters, is written in terms that Dryden or Joseph Addison might well have approved. It emerges again in T. S. Eliot's regret that William Blake's capacities were not "controlled by a respect for impersonal reason, for common sense, for the objectivity of science," and by "a framework of accepted and traditional ideas. . . ." [1] Eliot's very language approaches the neoclassical, and we recall that he too held Virgil in high esteem.

In the chapters that follow I have not hesitated to express a personal opinion on several aspects of neoclassical critical theory and practice. In extenuation of what may seem presumptuous to some, I can only say that my purpose in doing so has been far less to win converts, or to "set the record straight," than to suggest how much there is in what the generations of Dryden, Alexander Pope, and Samuel Johnson thought about literature that is still worth taking seriously. My obligations to modern neoclassical scholarship will be obvious throughout, and beyond what is acknowledged in the few notes. Of one debt, however, it is needful and pleasant to make special mention: that owed to the students of English 0705, Wayne State University, who during the fall and winter of 1965–1966 helped me explore many of the topics to which this book is addressed.

I am also grateful to Wayne State University for generously awarding me a Faculty Research Fellowship for the summer of 1966, which greatly eased and expedited my task.

E. R. M.

Royal Oak, Michigan
April, 1967

Contents

THE POETICS OF REASON

I THE INTELLECTUAL SETTING

Any description of the neoclassical period should begin with the warning that it was not all of a piece. Almost all its characteristic values, most of which had crystallized before 1700, were revised, challenged, and in some cases reversed during the eighteenth century. This generalization holds more for England than for France, where neoclassicism received its first and purest formulation and where it persisted longer. There, the great creative work of Corneille, Molière, La Fontaine, and especially Racine followed and largely conformed to a classicism whose main tenets had been established by Jean Chapelain and others around 1640 and were attractively and influentially codified in Boileau's *Art poétique* (1674). Imported into England, French classical doctrines had somehow to be reconciled with an existing native literature that obviously clashed with them in important respects. This initial situation combined with other forces, some of them latent in the aesthetic itself, to produce the dynamic and evolutionary quality that distinguishes its English development.

From the outset English critics faced a dilemma. That Racine's *Athalie* was not *Hamlet* was no matter. They might even have been undisturbed by Shakespeare's disregard for the dramatic unities and the rules of decorum.

Their patriotism alone was often enough to excuse him, as one is reminded by Addison's quip that "Our inimitable Shakespear is a Stumbling-block to the whole tribe of these rigid Criticks." But Addison's complacency tends to obscure the fact that in many instances the Englishman who loved Shakespeare also genuinely admired and gave intellectual assent to the ideas promulgated so triumphantly in Louis XIV's France.

Several things conspired to make it so. Like the French, the English Restoration writer venerated the ancient critical documents—Aristotle's *Poetics,* Horace's *Ars Poetica,* and later Longinus' *On the Sublime*—of which the French system was professedly an extension and refinement. More important, that system struck Englishmen as in accord with the deepest intellectual currents of the time. In its stress on reason, order, and clarity Boileau's *Art poétique* seemed a kind of literary counterpart to René Descartes' *Discourse on Method.* The critics' very addiction to prescriptive rules, answering neatly enough to the geometer's axioms, accorded with the pervasive mathematicism that Descartes' philosophy had engendered. Thomas Rymer's comparison of Aristotle's rules to those governing a triangle became a critical commonplace still being echoed a century later by Gotthold Lessing in Germany. Rules, after all, imply order, and order more than anything else was the watchword of the age. Order—in the universe, in the state, in the individual soul—was what that age mainly thirsted for and what for a time at least it came to believe in. "Order is Heaven's first law," Pope wrote in *An Essay on Man.* For this reason, one can endorse René Bray's conclusion that the dramatic unities of action, time, and place owe their final triumph not to any single critic but to the age itself.[1]

On the eve of the Restoration the longing for order was as strong in England as anywhere else. Englishmen were weary of strife and ready to welcome the peace of certainty in place of the clash of opinions in politics, in religion, and in every branch of secular thought. In the preface to his *Poems* (1656), Abraham Cowley voiced a common complaint against the turbulence of the times, "the best to write of, but the worst to *write in*," years in which, as the young Dryden was shortly to remark, Englishmen were so unruly that they hadn't leisure to be good poets.

Apart from this yearning for order, though no doubt subtly related to it, was a change in English literary taste that made for a ready acceptance of French critical ideas. Before Boileau, in the second Canto of his *Art*, satirized the conceited style (*pointes*) and the use of puns in prose and verse (*"chaque mot eut toujours deux images divers"* —each word always had two distinct meanings), English critics had already condemned them. In both countries there arose a distaste for the intricate and the florid and for that ingenious playing with and on words that marks the verse of the metaphysical poets and the prose of Sir Thomas Browne. Boileau relegated mere sallies of wit to the epigram, lowliest of the genres, and insisted that even there they ought to turn on the thought, not on the sound of the words. When Addison later castigated the exploitation of the similarities between words apart from their meanings as a species of "false wit," in *Spectator* 62, he was mainly providing a basis in Lockean psychology for condemning a stylistic device that his more informed readers already disliked. It is the same with that other type of his false wit best known in the examples by George Herbert, stanzas shaped to look like organs, hatchets, altars, and wings. The philosopher Thomas Hobbes in 1650 had already animadverted on this practice.[2] Boileau's call for reason and imaginative restraint must have seemed mild enough to those who had read Bishop Thomas Sprat's *History of the Royal Society* (1667), in which the author went so far as to excoriate as a hindrance to science "this vicious abundance of phrase, this trick of metaphors. . . ."

Yet the English debt to French literary speculation must not be minimized. During the years of the Commonwealth the English court, with its retinue of wits and *literati*, had lived in France. Most educated Englishmen read French and some of them translated contemporary French critical writings. Augustan English critical essays bristle with allusions and appeals to French authority. Dryden's debt to Pierre Corneille's *Discours* (1660) and *Examens* (1660) is well known. Rymer, who translated René Rapin's *Réflexions sur la poétique d'Aristote* in 1674, derived his concept of character decorum almost *verbatim* from Jules de la Mesnardière's *La Poétique* (1639) and regarded André Dacier and René Le Bossu as the reformers of modern poetry. Some French critical treatises were read in London almost as soon as they were in Paris. John Dennis' first important piece of criticism, *The Impartial Critic* (1693), contains a refutation of the defense of the tragic chorus that appeared in André Dacier's translation of Aristotle's *Poetics* published in the previous year. Even during the eighteenth century, when British literary thought became increasingly independent of Continental influence, many French critics continued to enjoy high repute. Pope, whose *An Essay on Criticism* (1711) somewhat sneeringly reminded his countrymen that "critic learning flourished most in France," later paid René Le Bossu's influential *Traité du poème épique* (1675) the compliment of parody in his *Peri Bathous, or of the Art of Sinking in Poetry* (1728). *La Manière de bien penser dans les ouvrages d'esprit* (1687) by Dominique Bouhours, paraphrased in George Granville's *Essay upon Unnatural Flights in Poetry* in 1701 and Englished in 1705 "by a person of quality," was thereafter frequently cited. Addison considered Bouhours "the most penetrating" of French critics. Jean-Baptiste Dubos' important *Réflexions critiques sur la poésie et la peinture* (1719) earned the deserved tribute of English translation by Thomas Nugent in 1748, and was often cited, as for example by David Hume and the Wartons and even as late as 1789 by Thomas Twining. Boileau, influential from the start, continued to be regarded in England almost on a par with ancient classical authority well into the century. In 1756 Joseph Warton rated his *Art poétique* as the finest art of poetry extant.

But the list is endless. It must not however be allowed to derogate from the originality of the English achievement. What is perhaps the most just assessment of the debt to France was made recently by a French student of English Augustan literary criticism, who concludes that his country's main contribution lay in the order of dialectic, in providing an orderly method and a critical terminology.[3]

Recent scholarship has shown that during the English Enlightenment literature and society, thought and feeling, aspiration and achievement were in fact less harmoniously adjusted than was once thought. But if the desired order and symmetry were often hardly won and precariously held, in contrast to later cultural eras there was at least a common feeling that they were not outside the range of human capacity. The faith that a correspondence between inner and outer worlds might be realized was based on the assurance that the universe was in fact harmonious. The new science, culminating in Sir Isaac Newton's *Principia* (1687), removed all doubt that this was so for the physical universe, as later in the same decade John Locke's *Essay Concerning Human Understanding* (1690) seemed to establish it for the microcosm. The achievement of these men argued strongly for the mutual adjustment of reason and nature; the laws of a demonstrably regular universe were knowable. Even those who were shortly to exalt the faculty of taste above reason in aesthetic experience were confident that the Almighty had so constituted the human mind that external beauty "should make a responsive harmony vibrate within," as John Gilbert Cooper expressed it in *Letters Concerning Taste* (1755). If a corresponding order did not, or not yet, prevail in the arts, that was owing to human ignorance or perversity. "For harmony is harmony by nature," wrote the Earl of Shaftesbury in his

Advice to an Author (1710). "So is symmetry and proportion founded still in nature, let men's fancy prove
ever so barbarous, or their fashions ever so Gothic in
their architecture, sculpture, or whatever other designing
art."

The typical contemporary description of literary excellence and how to attain or judge it comprises a small
set of terms either identical with or obviously correlative
to the crucial abstractions defining the moral and physical
worlds: reason, nature, symmetry, proportion, regularity.
Thus Boileau's

> *Aimez donc la raison, que toujours vos écrits*
> *Empruntent d'elle seule leur lustre et leur prix;**

or Pope's "First follow Nature," which is "At once the
source, and end, and test of art," along with that other
passage from *An Essay on Criticism* that so eloquently
epitomizes the Augustan conception of artistic beauty and
unity:

> *'Tis not a lip or eye we beauty call,*
> *But the joint force and full result of all.*
> *Thus when we view some well-proportioned dome,*
> *(The world's just wonder, and even thine, O Rome!)*
> *No single parts unequally surprise,*
> *All comes united to th' admiring eyes;*
> *No monstrous height, or breadth, or length appear;*
> *The whole at once is bold, and regular;*

or Dr. Johnson's "Nothing can please many or please long
but just representations of general nature."

Objection *ad nauseam* has been made that the key
terms "reason" and "nature" shift sense from one context
to another. It is even alleged that "nature" and "the
natural" have so many various referents during this period as to elude all definition. Although this opinion is
obscurantist nonsense, it is true that these grand abstractions feebly convey a notion of what readers actually

* Love Reason then, and always let your writings borrow their
beauty and value from her.

liked or disliked in a poem. Taken seriously, some of their dearest maxims seem to a modern understanding downright puzzling, like the idea that good (or common) sense is an essential quality in poetry. We may feel it to be equally true to say that poetry deals with uncommon sense, assuming it is an affair of sense at all in the usual acceptance of the term. To come at a more just idea of their taste, it is therefore best to turn to a few examples of what writers specifically praised or blamed, a process that also helps to define the vague terms they used to express it.

But first a warning. To understand the literary taste of a past age (in contradistinction to its theory) requires an imaginative sharing of that taste never fully attainable. The most sympathetic modern appreciation of what the readers of Dryden or Pope sought and relished in play or poem has always to reckon with an irreducible gap of sensibility between those readers and ourselves. Even similarity of judgment does not necessarily mean identity of response. The increasing praise of Shakespeare throughout the eighteenth century cannot conceal the fact that many of the very things in his work that are considered most attractive today were positively distasteful then. *Hamlet* was accorded the same high rank that it has now, but almost everything written on it at that time reminds us of the considerable difference between the object of their appreciation and that of our own. We have a glimpse of this in the "improvement" proposed by one admirer of the play, the actor Francis Gentleman. In his *Dramatic Censor* (1770), Gentleman suggested that Shakespeare would have done better to have Claudius divulge his plan to kill Hamlet to the Queen, who then warns her son, who in turn takes proper countermeasures. In this way Claudius would have been shown a consistent tyrant, Gertrude a tender mother, and Hamlet a hero. Best of all the innocent Polonius and Ophelia would have been spared, and "death prevented from stalking, without limitation, at the catastrophe. . . ." Gentleman's writings give the impression that he was a bit of an ass, but there is no reason to suppose that many of his readers thought his emendation assinine.

In 1725 Pope did not hesitate to laud Shakespeare as the instrument rather than the mere imitator of nature. Yet three years later in *Peri Bathous* he finds these lines from *The Tempest* "cumbrous":

> *Advance the fringed curtains of thy eyes*
> *And tell me who comes yonder. . . .*

At best we may understand his point, but without sharing his objection, much as we see what he *means* by his example of mixed metaphor: "an ingenious Artist painting the Spring, talks of a *Snow of Blossoms,* and thereby raises an unexpected picture of Winter." Yet the image doesn't really shock us, especially if we recall Housman's

> *About the woodlands I will go*
> *To see the cherry hung with snow.*[4]

Dr. Johnson's praise of Shakespeare is even greater than Pope's and better grounded. Still, he finds the soliloquies, which he calls set pieces, "cold and weak," whereas they seem to us unsurpassed in their emotive power. It was once common to ascribe remarks of this kind to an alleged insensitivity to poetry on Johnson's part (himself a poet!). But we know he was moved to tears by Pope's poetry and in his great edition of Shakespeare's plays he observed that a reader of Macbeth's description of the evils that stalk the night "looks round alarmed, and starts to find himself alone."

The clearest indices to the change in taste that accompanied the emergence of a new poetic idiom and facilitated the triumph of neoclassical literary theory in England are at first mainly negative, expressions of scorn for the harsh language and the fanciful imagery of the earlier seventeenth century. John Donne was admired more as wit than as poet. Abraham Cowley, the last of the metaphysicals, enjoyed a high but declining reputation. "Who now reads Cowley?" Pope could ask in 1737,

> *if he pleases yet,*
> *His Moral pleases, not his pointed wit.*

Dryden, born in 1631, actually lived through the alteration of poetic idiom and taste which by precept and example he helped to bring about. He provides a revealing instance of the kind of conceited style grown repugnant by 1680. In youth he had admired Sylvester's couplet:

> *To glaze the lakes, to bridle up the floods,*
> *And periwig with snow [wool] the bald-pate woods.*

Now he considers it "fustian," the diction and thought mutually ill-suited.

Two poets of the previous generation, Edmund Waller and Sir John Denham, were widely admired as happy exceptions. Waller was regarded as a pioneer in the reform of English versification. Dryden acknowledged his tutelage in this regard; Rymer declared that English "did not shine and sparkle till Mr. *Waller* set it a running"; Dennis credited him with teaching his countrymen to appreciate "the Musick of a just Cadence." A preference for Waller was considered a mark of modern refinement. Dorimant, the hero of Sir George Etherege's highly popular comedy *The Man of Mode* (1676), constantly quotes his love verses. As for Denham, one couplet of his *Cooper's Hill,* endlessly quoted, served as a virtual touchstone that expressed and exemplified the Augustan ideals of clarity, sweetness, and smoothness:

> *Though deep, yet clear: though gentle yet not dull,*
> *Strong without rage; without o'erflowing full.*

Nothing so fine as this, it was thought, had ever been written in English.

It is instructive to look beneath the often irritating condescension toward their literary predecessors to see what, exactly, the Restoration critics objected to in poetic language. A good example is John Dennis' critique of Waller's poem *To the King on His Navy,* in the third dialogue of his *Impartial Critic.* Here are the notions that poetry ought to be as perspicuous and as grammatically correct as prose and that there are distinct levels of poetic diction. Even the admired Waller is found insufficiently "correct." His syntax is faulty and his metaphors mixed. Some words are too "mean" for heroic verse: *fray, speed, fishes.* Most interesting is Dennis' exception to *heretofor* as obsolete. The prosodic refinement had placed this and similar adverbial conjunctives under special ban. Robert Wolseley, in his preface to the Earl of Rochester's *Valentinian,* supplies a long list of them, and Shaftesbury, otherwise critical of contemporary poets, admits that they have at least "reformed in some measure the gouty joints and darning-work of *whereunto's, whereby's, thereof's, therewith's,* and the rest of this kind. . . ." Clearly the implied criterion here is as much efficiency as simplicity, every word to count, and these locutions were often as useless as they were graceless. A like motive prompts Dryden's disparagement of expletives in *An Essay of Dramatic Poesy,* duly echoed in *An Essay on Criticism* by Pope, who in a letter to Henry Cromwell dubs them "mere fillers-up of unnecessary syllables."

The critical commentaries on Shakespeare and Milton are useful but somewhat deceptive indicators of neoclassical literary attitudes. Neither writer answered very readily to the Augustan ideal at its strictest and most exclusive. The growing reputation of both throughout the entire period parallels the gradual dilution of that ideal, just as it was a major causal factor in the evolution of its critical theory. It is Virgil who provides the most accurate guide to the common denominator of taste that justifies our applying a single label to a century and a half of literary history. Awed by Homer's brilliance, and stirred by their worship of the epic genre to emulate its Greek founder in various ways, neoclassical writers really

found Virgil more to their liking. At once sublime and
urbane, the Roman poet perfectly embodied in his work
what they most admired in technique, style, and genre.
He was "heroic" *and* civilized; he was a conscious craftsman; he wrote admirable didactic verse. He was, in Dennis' words, "the best of Poets and the justest of Writers."
Sir Richard Blackmore, who took the *Aeneid* as the
model for his unfortunate heroic poems on Prince and
King Arthur, rightly considered Virgil more accommo-
dated to "the present age" than Homer. Dryden translated the *Aeneid* and repeatedly professed his profound
admiration of its author. Addison's first critical essay was
an appreciation of the *Georgics.* Pope anonymously defended his own youthful *Pastorals,* in *Guardian* 40, by
ironically deploring their similarity to the Virgilian *Ec-
logues.*

The relaxation of the earliest neoclassical poetic only
very gradually affected this universal love for Virgil. The
Longinian Joseph Trapp declared in his Oxford lectures
on poetry (1711–1719) that he knew no masterpiece in
art or nature greater than Dido's lament in Book IV of
the *Aeneid.* In 1756 Joseph Warton, whose poetry and
criticism alike successfully challenged the standards that
predominated during the age of Pope, described a passage in the third *Georgic* as "moving beyond compare."

Horace, that other ornament of the envied reign of the
emperor Augustus, enjoyed a comparable vogue. His verse
satires and epistles, and above all his highly finished odes
and epodes, many of them extolling the virtues of common sense and a life of decorous hedonism, seemed the
embodiment *par excellence* of his own injunction to poets
to file and polish their work. Pope, a kindred spirit in his
devotion to the labor of the file, was chief among those
who wrote "imitations" of Horatian satire. Constantly
cited as unimpeachable authority, Horace's *Epistle to
the Pisos* (often titled the *Ars Poetica*) was for a time
taken as the sum of critical wisdom. Dryden's critical
essays are dotted with tags from this long overrated work,

which also provided Addison, Steele, and Dr. Johnson with epigraphs for several *Spectator* and *Adventurer* papers. Yet as a poet Horace was ranked below Virgil, who after all had written an epic, supreme among the poetic kinds. If he was not, like Horace, a satiric poet, it is still worth noting that the greatest verse satire of this satire-loving age, Pope's *Dunciad,* parodies the *Aeneid.* And as the eighteenth century advanced, Horace's authority as a critic yielded gradually to that of Longinus. By 1756 Joseph Warton was attacking as nonsense the "vulgar notion" that the *Epistle to the Pisos* constituted a complete poetics. Horace's poetry Warton characterized as elegant, not sublime, a reservation to which Virgil, whose works Warton had translated and edited in 1753, was largely immune. Virgil had everything. "His talents," Bishop Hurd observed, "were, indeed, universal."

But the concept of taste involved something far more profound than a mere preference for one style or author over another. At this time as in others since, taste in the arts was conceived by the most sensitive minds as symptomatic of social and moral health. The tawdry poet was an uncivilizing force and a liking for his wares carried the threat of barbarism. Part of the *Spectator*'s reformist purpose was to check what Addison felt to be the "extremely Gothick" taste of most English poets and readers; and he was only half in jest in expressing his fear, in *Spectator* 61, that the growing rage for punning and acrostic verses might portend a kind of racial degeneracy. The Augustan critics' typical abuse of the Middle Ages and their patronizing attitude toward the Renaissance itself, so irritating to a modern reader, should not be misconstrued as a general complacency about their own day. Many were aware that the enlightenment they enjoyed had followed a long period of darkness and disorder that might well be brought back by pandering to a debased literary standard. This is a major motif of Pope's *Dunciad,* in which the Dunces are finally seen to be more dangerous than contemptible. In the perspective of literary history the Augustans' concern may seem unjustified. But the belief that "a deficiency of taste and a corruption of manners are sometimes found mutually to produce each other," as Oliver Goldsmith put it in *An Enquiry into the Present State of Polite Learning in Europe* (1759), persisted as a kind of unexamined dogma throughout much of the eighteenth century.

Although there is no denying the widespread contemporary satisfaction at the apparent victory of human rationality over the chaotic forces of prejudice and superstition, for the finest minds of the Age of Reason, reason itself was double-edged. Sole guarantor of order, civilization, and good taste, reason could be so perverted, as in the case of Swift's "civilized" European Yahoos, as to produce a barbarism far blacker than the innocent barbarism of the Yahoos in Houyhnhnmland. Gulliver's fleeting recognition that a tincture of intelligence served only to substitute firearms and cutlasses for the Yahoos' claws and fangs is a glance into the heart of darkness as sobering as those given us later by Dostoevsky's underground man or Conrad's Mr. Kurtz. Analogously in the realm of art, the touch of pride, envy, or vanity could convert a wise love of what is beautiful or sound into a purblind hankering after the meretricious. In each case the antidote was a commitment not to Descartes' pure reason but to the Right Reason of the Christian humanist. Pope's Dunces were

> *Of naught so certain as our* Reason *still,*
> *Of naught so doubtful as of* Soul *and* Will.

The pedant was as deleterious as the Grub-street hack. "The bookful blockhead" of *An Essay on Criticism* was guilty of divorcing letters from social usefulness. "Forever reading, never to be read," as the *Dunciad* described him, he spread a kind of sterility blight in the kingdom of letters. In a verse epistle on *Taste* published in 1753, John Armstrong was still displaying his feeble wit at the expense of

> *thousands of scholastic merit*
> *Who worm their sense out but ne'er taste their spirit.*
> *Witness each pedant under Bentley bred;*
> *Each commentator that e'er commented.*

But the term pedant was used too inclusively, employed as a chain shot against all scholarship whether sound or silly. The injustice of the satire directed against Richard Bentley's classical research is notorious. Nor could the editorial pioneering of Lewis Theobald's textual restorations of Shakespeare prevent his election as king of Pope's Dunces. Personal pique aside (Theobald had attacked Pope's own edition of Shakespeare), the underlying motive was a distrust of "empirics" and "virtuosi" in all fields of human endeavor, the same which led to Swift's indiscriminate ridicule of experimental science in *Gulliver's Travels.* Dr. Johnson, himself for a time a learned drudge, was more tolerant of commentators, editors, and the like, and defended the virtuoso in *Rambler* 83; but the Tory wits of Queen Anne's reign seemed mainly blind to the virtues of any philology but that in which they occasionally indulged themselves. Johnson was probably right when he remarked in the *Life of Pope* that that poet's attitude owed something to his pretense of being a spirit above such lowly labors.

The wits were even blinder—or deafer—to the Italian opera. Puritans of the previous age had attacked the stage in language scarcely more intemperate than that used by English neoclassic critics (Dryden notably excepted) against this increasingly popular importation. Contemplating its great vogue in France, Rymer cried "farewell Apollo and the Muses!" Dennis in 1711 declared that it had driven good taste and poetry itself out of England. In *The Complete Art of Poetry* (1718), Charles Gildon put opera in the same class with farce and Japanese pictures, as instances of a Gothic taste for the unnatural. Addison, himself the author of an unsuccessful opera entitled *Rosamond,* staged and printed in 1707, was at least willing to discuss the new art but disapproved of its appeal to sound in place of sense. His Aristotelian condemnation of its dependence on spectacle rather than on thought was widely endorsed. Gradually the general prejudice against opera subsided and was largely confined to the Italian form of it. In Book IV of the *Dunciad* it is specifically Italian opera that appears as a "Harlot form" in a passage that pictures the naturalized George Frederick Handel in vain and heroic opposition to the seductive foreigner. Much later in the century Adam Smith found nothing more moving than the combination of Metastasio's poetry, Pergolesi's melodies, and good acting; and Dr. Johnson was forced to admit in his declining years that this "exotic and irrational entertainment" had prevailed despite all opposition.

Of more lasting concern was the state of the English language. Ever since Elizabeth's time Englishmen had wondered whether their native tongue was a fit instrument for great literary expression. Dryden died in the conviction that it could not rival Latin, though he thought it superior to other modern languages for poetry. Still more alarming was its fluid condition. By the late seventeenth century it had become habitual to regret that since English was constantly changing nothing written in it would be readable a century or so after the author's death. English poets despaired of lasting fame, and some had their work translated into enduring Latin. All gloomily pondered Waller's depressing lines in *Of English Verse*:

> But who can hope his lines should long
> Last in a daily changing tongue?
>
> .   .   .
>
> Poets that lasting marble seek,
> Must carve in Latin, or in Greek.

Sir William Temple voiced the same complaint; so did Dryden, Pope, and others. With some, the need to arrest the process, to "ascertain" the language, became almost an obsession. Defoe and Swift advocated the founding of an academy for the purpose, as the French had done. Fortunately nothing came of these proposals, since, as Dr. Johnson later observed in the Preface to his *Dictionary* (1755), no such device could absolutely prevent linguistic change. And in any case, as he wryly observed in the *Lives of the English Poets* (1779–1781), Englishmen would make a point of disobeying any rules of usage emanating from an academy. Insofar as the language was stabilized at all, the task was accomplished by the dictionaries and grammars.

There was something else however. Not even Dr. Johnson shared Leonard Welsted's opinion of 1724 that "the most beautiful polish is at length given to our tongue, and its Teutonic rust quite worn away." In *Rambler* 88, he repeated an old charge that English suffered from an overplus of monosyllables. Critics had long been disturbed by this reminder of the barbaric, Gothic ancestry of the language. An apparent increase in the number of monosyllables partly resulting from the English habit of contracting words was therefore widely regarded as a harbinger of degeneracy as alarming as the taste for "false wit" or the Italian opera. In 1693 Dryden feared that "in a few years we shall speak as barbarously as our neighbors." In *Tatler* 230 (1710) Swift, announcing that the corruption of English was in full career, pointed to recent usages "altogether of a *Gothick* Strain," and to "a natural Tendency towards relapsing into Barbarity, which delighteth in monosyllables . . . when we are already overloaded with monosyllables." In the following year Addison deplored in *Spectator* 135 the disfigurement of the tongue caused by contracting *drowned* to *drown'd*, *walked* to *walk'd*, and so forth.

Today the spectacle of the very masters who perfected English prose lamenting the poor state and worse future of their language may seem amusing. Certainly Swift's disgust with modish priests who substituted "pardons and absolves" for the "pardoneth and absolveth" of the Absolution in the Service of Morning Prayer will strike most modern Anglicans as quaint and (as it turned out) needless. But the vital dependence of a culture on the health of its language must be ranked high among neo-classical intellectual legacies. The idea has in fact been confirmed in our own time by T. S. Eliot in *The Social Function of Poetry* and *Notes toward the Definition of Culture,* and dramatized by George Orwell in *1984.* The distortion of reality and the debasement of values, whether unconscious or by design, effected by the cloudy prose of many politicians, businessmen, and English professors are matters of daily witness by educated men and women. No scheme to cure this ailment ought to leave out of account the eighteenth-century conviction that speech conditions thought and thought morals. An unspoken assumption of much neoclassical thinking was that a graceful style is a sign of grace, a truth since obscured by the prostitution of language to the venal aims of mass advertising and political propaganda.

Other assumptions and attitudes about literature predominant in early neoclassicism are constantly reflected in the critical writing. By comparison with other times, neoclassical literature is markedly social and urban. Though he starved in a Paris slum or a Grub-street garret, the poet felt himself a part of society, not, like his Bohemian romantic counterpart, in proud rebellion against it. The proper source of his diction was not Wordsworth's countryside but the polite world of court and city. A writer stood to profit by commerce with well-bred men of the world rather than by solitary communion with nature. Bishop Sprat wrote that the qualities of mind and expression that make good poetry were derived mainly from "frequent conversation in cities," and he praised Cowley for having withdrawn from society without dropping the language of city and court. Molière's Dorante, in *La critique de l'Ecole des femmes,* affirmed that in matters of literary taste the natural good sense of *le beau monde* was preferable to the rusty erudition of pedants.

Though the pedant might be learned, he was not a gentleman. The ideal was versified in the Earl of Roscommon's widely read *Essay on Translated Verse* (1684):

> *For none have been with Admiration read*
> *But who, beside their* learning, *were* Well-bred.

The playwright Thomas Shadwell held that poets could best avoid assigning rough and ill-bred speech to their tragic characters by attending to the conversation of courts. Wolseley ascribed the qualities of good breeding and "gentlemen-like easiness" in Rochester's poetry to his having been reared at court. Looking back at the Elizabethan poets, Dryden regretted that their wit was not that of gentlemen, since none of them except Ben Jonson had moved in aristocratic circles. Like so many other norms entertained by the Augustans, this was to be abandoned in the later decades of the neoclassical era. Yet as late as 1725 Pope was amazed to find pertinent and judicious reflections in Shakespeare, who, as he thought, lacked experience of "those great and public scenes of life" depicted in his plays. Shakespeare's use of inappropriately mean diction in *Macbeth* (*dun, knife, blanket*) led Dr. Johnson in *Rambler* 168 to place early entrance into society among the requirements for successful authorship, since the graces of language could be gotten only from "general converse."

Whatever else may now be said of it, this view of the relation between literature and society was quite consistent with the doctrine of imitating nature. For Dryden, Pope, and Johnson, nature was primarily human nature, and neoclassical humanism is essentially a socialized humanism. Johnson's distaste for pastoral poetry rests in part on the inherent limitation of the rural scene. The shepherd's ambition, he observed in 1750, "is without policy, and his love without intrigue." He suffers no disasters more interesting than the cruelties of a mistress or a crop failure. The nonhuman nature later worshiped by the Romantics, which the pastoral *could* exploit, Johnson dismissed as "mere" nature.

As suggested above, many of the attitudes and notions so far discussed were radically redefined or reversed before the end of the eighteenth century. The initially pejorative "Gothic," for example, gradually became a term of approval. Similarly with "enthusiastic." Enthusiasm, in 1655 the subject of a treatise by Meric Casaubon, in earlier neoclassical writing denoted everything in religion, politics, and literature that was exorbitant, idiosyncratic, ultra-fanciful—in a word, "unnatural." In *Absalom and Achitophel* (1681) Dryden reveals its essential import and flavor in his brief "character" of Puritans:

> *A numerous Host of dreaming Saints succeed;*
> *Of the true old Enthusiastick Breed:*
> *'Gainst Form and Order they their Pow'r imploy;*
> *Nothing to Build, and all Things to Destroy.*

By the middle of the next century, however, "enthusiasm," like its semantic companions "Gothic" and "romantic," had achieved the generally honorific connotation it has since retained. Well before this process was complete the word had been used, with hesitant approval, to denote the irrational element in artistic creation. In 1711 Shaftesbury, not surprisingly, detected in poetic rapture what he is careful to distinguish as a *plausible* enthusiasm, as, even earlier, William Wotton had defended the poet's "enthusiastick" rage. But these were then minority voices.

The evolution of literary taste and critical theory signaled by these and other semantic shifts will be treated in a later chapter. In the meantime it will be useful to reaffirm the well-justified caution of modern neoclassical scholarship against labeling these tendencies romanticism. There is no harm in calling certain attitudes expressed by Shaftesbury, or by the Wartons or Hurd later on, *pre*romantic, in the sense that they contributed to an intellectual atmosphere favorable to the emergence of romanticism itself. We know that Wordsworth acknowledged his poetic debt to Bishop Percy's *Reliques* (1765) and found something congenial even in Dennis. Inevitable links of this kind between the two centuries must not however lead us to overlook the strong evidence that men of the eighteenth century would scarcely have comprehended, let alone approved, the main tenets of the romantic critical program. Though this is not the place to review that evidence, an illustration may suggest the necessary discrimination. Shaftesbury's "romanticism" is said to reveal itself most notably in his appreciation of natural scenery. Yet in *The Moralists* the language in which Theocles confesses his love for the wilderness manifests the attitudinal distance separating Shaftesbury and the romantic celebrants of mountain and forest. He speaks of "*rude* rocks . . . *irregular unwrought* grottoes and *broken* falls of waters, with all the *horrid* graces of the wilderness. . . ." His words no doubt evince a kind of love for natural beauty; but it is not Wordsworth's kind, nor Keats'. It belongs to its own age.

Quite apart from the alterations which neoclassical critical thought underwent in the course of time are certain theoretical ambivalences, and some discrepancies between criticism and practice, prevalent at any given moment. These deserve notice for what they reveal of the dynamism and restless quality of a period of English literary history often regarded, in its Augustan heyday, as essentially static and intellectually at peace with itself. The general belief of the age was that art like everything else was subject to laws which a would-be practitioner ought to know and abide by. Yet arguments for the indispensability of the critical rules are matched by others—often in the same critic—damning them, or some of them, as useless. Dennis calls them "eternal and invincible." Leonard Welsted mocks them. Addison in 1712 opined that a writer sometimes shows more judgment in violating than in following the rules, but in 1713 produced his absurdly regular tragedy *Cato*. And it was

Dennis who demonstrated its absurdity in an analysis later approved by Dr. Johnson. Any attempt at a neat division of critics into those for and those against the rules is defeated by facts like these and by the further complication that even the staunchest apologists for regularity were at odds among themselves as to what in fact the true rules were.

Other contradictions are subtler and harder to assess in their total impact. The most gifted figures of an age distinguished chiefly for its comic and satirical writing admired epic poetry above all. A few, like Dryden, aspired to write it. Cowley and Davenant tried and failed. (Milton's obvious success was slow to be recognized as such.) Most, like Dryden and Pope, satisfied the itch through parody or translation. "I should certainly have written an Epick Poem," Pope told his friend Joseph Spence, "if I had not engaged in the translation of Homer." All believed, as Pope observed in *Peri Bathous,* that an epic poem was the greatest work possible to the human mind. The widespread critical approval of the emphasis placed on common sense and rational expression by Boileau and Sprat is balanced by frequent pleas for imaginative freedom. Boileau himself is said to have complained that Descartes had cut poetry's throat. Dryden vigorously defended poetic license. Even Thomas Rymer, though apparently deaf to Shakespeare's verbal music, could be eloquent in defense of metaphor. Homer, he wrote in the *Short View of Tragedy* (1692), appeals by trope and figure to "our Eyes, our Ears, our Touch; *Nectar* he provides for our Taste, and there always exhales an ambrosial Odour in the Divine Presence." No philosopher, he continues, not Plato himself, could so affect us, because "Metaphor must be the Language, when we travel in a Countrey beyond our Senses." For their time and place, such declarations may seem daring; yet behind them lay the comforting authority of Aristotle's dictum that the mark of a poet is the ability to make metaphors.

A further ambivalence of stylistic taste exists in the demand for simplicity along with a love for elegant ornamentation in the arts. Dennis went so far as to declare "the most pompous Eloquence" not inconsistent with "Simplicity of Style." What in fact did the Augustans mean by "simplicity"? Much that we should call simple they decried as mean or "low." Addison rightly feared that his praise for the ballad of *Chevy Chase* would be laughed at, as it was by Dennis and even by Dr. Johnson in his *Life of Addison*. Confirming Dennis, Johnson declared that though admittedly devoid of bombast the old ballad was marred by "chill and lifeless imbecility." Knowing and in some sort sharing the prevalent taste, Addison had warned his readers not to let the "simplicity of the style" prejudice them against the nobility of the thought. But in vain. His ballad papers continued to occasion burlesque mockery for a decade after their appearance.

In the Preface to his translation of the *Iliad* (1715), Pope defined simplicity as the mean between ostentation and rusticity, and we recall his contempt in *An Essay on Criticism* for poets who "hide with ornaments their want of art." On the other hand, no one during the entire period seriously challenged Richard Hurd's assumption in 1765 that poetry of whatever kind involved "a choice of such words as are sonorous and expressive, and such an arrangement of them as throws the discourse out of the ordinary and common phrase of conversation." There was, one must suppose, a kind of ornamentation that was not ostentatious, though it may be difficult to reconcile it with any ideal to which the word *simple* would be appropriate. Even assuming the possibility of some such accommodation on the conceptual level, we are left with an apparent discrepancy between the poetry written at the time and any conceivable interpretation of the theory. Against whatever Pope *meant* in the Preface to the *Iliad*, we have to place what he often *did* in the translation. In one of the two dissertations *On Poetry*,

Considered as an Imitative Art prefixed to his edition of Aristotle's *Poetics* (1789), Thomas Twining noted that Homer's single adjective "grassy" becomes in Pope's version

> . . . *grassy Pteleon deck'd with cheerful greens,*
> *The bow'rs of Ceres and the sylvan scenes.*

Nevertheless, it seems better to describe the relation between critical theory and poetic practice as one of tension rather than outright contradiction. Dr. Johnson could admire Pope's facility in decorating his ideas with the graces of elegant expression, as he has it in the *Life of Pope;* yet he certainly shared Pope's disapproval of ostentation, cautioning in *Idler* 36 against the deliberate straining after elegance that destroys clarity and perspicuity. Still, elegance and ceremony in manners, speech, and everything else were hallmarks of the age. Addison noted with satisfaction in his essay on Virgil's *Georgics* that the Roman poet even tossed dung in a graceful manner.

In any case, what is simple need not be barren. "Simplicity," wrote Sir Joshua Reynolds, "when so very inartificial as to seem to evade the difficulties of art, is a very suspicious virtue." Lovers of another great neoclassical artist, W. A. Mozart, attest readily enough to their experience of simplicity subsisting in elegant variation.

II *THE NEOCLASSICAL AESTHETIC*

MIMESIS

When in 1772 the learned Orientalist Sir William Jones published an essay entitled *On the Arts Commonly Called Imitative,* denying that poetry and music produced their proper effects by imitation, he was striking at the central principle of neoclassical literary theory. Amid the many changes of doctrine and emphasis that had enlivened literary debate since the dawn of modern criticism in Renaissance Italy, the mimetic conception of the nature of art had gone virtually unquestioned. "It is justly considered as the greatest excellency of art to imitate nature," wrote Dr. Johnson in an early *Rambler* paper, with no fear that any reader would doubt it. And just four years earlier in France Charles Batteux, in *Les Beaux-Arts réduits à un même principe* (1746), had constructed a general theory for all the fine arts on the basis of their common mimetic function. Though rejected by some aestheticians today, the idea that the nexus between art and reality is in some sense imitative is still widely entertained on good evidence. For critics of the Renaissance and the Enlightenment there was the added backing of Aristotle's assertion that art imitates nature.

How did neoclassical writers conceive of literary imitation? Certainly neither then nor at any time since has universal acceptance of the doctrine baldly stated guaranteed unanimity as to its meaning and implications. For the seventeenth and eighteenth centuries, however, two generalizations may be fairly made. Few if any critics subscribed to the naive representationism (art as mimicry) that was the real object of Jones' attack and that he incorrectly fathered upon Aristotle. With rare and doubtful exceptions, neither the notion that a poem is a direct reflection of "life" nor the notion that it is a wholly autonomous creation finds support in neoclassical theory. Poets did not feel bound to reproduce with unselective fidelity the perceptions of eye and ear. On the other hand neither did they think of their activity as analogous to the creativity of God or nature. Though the idea later evolved by romantic theorists that the artist imitates by repeating the Maker's creative process is certainly glimpsed in Shaftesbury's arresting image of the poet as "a second *maker*, a just Prometheus under Jove," his contemporaries seem never to have taken the hint, probably because it was fundamentally at odds with the predominantly empiricist-rationalist orientation of the age. It does, one should note, make a vague reappearance in Jones' piece when he argues that the artist attains his end by assuming nature's powers and affecting the imagination as natural beauty affects the senses.

Two terms, themselves of unfixed definition, delimit the neoclassical conception of mimesis: "probability" (or verisimilitude) and "nature." No rule, wrote Sir Richard Blackmore, was to be more "chastly" observed than probability. If the plot of his epic or tragedy was improbable, the poet failed to instruct. Granted, he must also delight, but few could forget Boileau's maxim that nothing was beautiful unless it was true.

True is what sense? The French theorists had taught that truth (*le vrai*) must be the aim of all art, but with the proviso that this truth itself had to stand the test of probability (*vraisemblance*). Poets impatient of being tied to bare possibilities were glad to recall Boileau's concession (wrenched from its qualifying context) that the true might sometimes be improbable. Such was the truth of the historian, bound to relate what happened however it might strain belief. Typically, critics insisted on a distinction between the historian's "truth narrative and past . . . a dead thing," as Davenant had characterized it in the Preface to *Gondibert* (1650), and "truth operative, and by its effects continually alive. . . ."

The reiterated pleas by creative writers for some degree of latitude in the definition of probability have to be read against the strong rationalist distrust of the imaginative and the fictive. In the Preface to his translation of Rapin's *Réflexions sur la poétique d'Aristote* (1674), Thomas Rymer condemned the lack of probability in Spenser's *The Faerie Queene,* dubbing the poem "perfect Fairy-land," and criticized Cowley's use of the "impossibilities" of miraculous Old Testament history in his *Davideis.* The epic poet more than any other, as Milton's nephew Edward Phillips wrote, ought to stick as close to the truth as possible. As late as 1762, in a chapter of his influential *Elements of Criticism* devoted to the emotions caused by fiction, Lord Kames protested against epic machinery as improbable and unreal. It would be wrong to dismiss these restrictions as the pronouncements of dull and doctrinaire theorists, since a sincere distaste for the merely fanciful, prior to all theory and more profound in its effects, was one of the characteristics of the time. Poem or play pleased as the reader saw in them some conformity to the requirements of logic or the actualities of experience. This peculiar commerce between truth and pleasure in the verbal arts had found perhaps its neatest expression under the heading of *Eloquence* in Blaise Pascal's *Pensées*: "Il faut de l'agréable et du réel; mais il faut que cet agréable soit lui-même pris du vrai"—Both the agreeable and the real are required; but this agreeable must itself be derived from truth. An age that delighted in truth in all things made no special provision for literature.

Even Addison's defense of the imaginary, in *Spectator* 419, is hardly an exception. It leaves no doubt that the "fairy way of writing" is an imposture violating the law of probability, admirable only because it flatters our natural prejudices. Only a year before, this same Addison had taught his subscribers that the basis of all wit was truth, and censured the allegorical figures of Sin and Death in *Paradise Lost* as insufficiently probable for an epic poem. Taken together, what he has to say on this issue, as on many others, epitomizes the Augustan position, which sought a compromise between the strictest naturalism and the license of ungoverned invention. An epic poem, many Restoration writers had felt, must be especially wary of the marvelous if it is to recommend itself seriously as a pattern of virtuous conduct. Admitting this, others had nonetheless repined at being held too closely within the bounds of the natural, arguing plausibly enough that Homer and Virgil, the great exemplars of the genre whom they were aspiring to emulate, had peopled their epics with supernatural beings and represented their heroes performing extraordinary actions. In his essay *Of Heroic Plays* (1672) Dryden pointed out that neither they nor the Italian epic poets Ariosto and Tasso could have written so beautifully "without those gods and spirits, and those enthusiastic [note the daring word] parts of poetry which compose the noblest parts of all their writings." His rather feeble plea that for all we know such unearthly beings may in fact exist reveals the central ambivalence of early neoclassical theory in its attempt to honor both classical precedent and contemporary rationalism. Addison allowed for both claims in *Spectator* 315: "If the fable is only probable, it differs nothing from a true History; if it is only marvellous, it is no better than a Romance."

That realism in the sense advocated in the next century

by an Emile Zola found few apologists at this time is
owing in large measure to the very different meaning
which the two centuries assigned to that "nature" which
the work of art was supposed to imitate. For Dryden,
Pope, and Johnson, nature was not the sum of experienced
phenomena, but rather, in its general acceptance, an
ideal system governed by laws to which any particular
object or event might imperfectly conform. Dennis gave
it a Neoplatonic formulation when he declared that the
poet was to imitate the universal idea implanted by the
Creator in every man's mind, not the imperfect copy of
that idea embodied in the particular. The most thorough-
going advocate of this kind of classical idealism was Sir
Joshua Reynolds, who in his third *Discourse on Art*
(1770) quoted and elaborated Proclus' statement that
the actual works of nature, being marred by disproportion,
fall short of the truly beautiful. It is only in a "confined
and misunderstood sense of the word" that the imitation
of circumstantial detail can be called natural, Reynolds
thought. Properly speaking, nature refers to the general
idea alone. More often though, theory held that the
artist followed nature by offering only what was most
decorous, life purged of the ugly, the painful, the dull,
as when Dr. Johnson wrote in the *Life of Shenstone* that
a pastoralist should display the beauties but not the
grossness of rural life. The poet's art was selection. In
fact, however, this simple formula inadequately describes
the actual practice of neoclassical poets, whose fictive
worlds are not so much combinations of choice features
taken from real life as variations on one or another
literary convention. "A pastoral," Pope wrote in the 1717
edition of his *Works*, "is an imitation of the action of a
shepherd"; but the actions of the ceremonious rustics
pictured in his *Pastorals* (1709) are such as no real shepherd ever performed. Pope knew—and knew that his
readers would know—that his business was to "illustrate"
an ancient genre, not to report on a branch of stock
raising.

What writers and their readers at any moment between the Restoration and the romantic period really felt to constitute a successful imitation of nature is best gleaned from the finest poems, plays, and novels, not from critical theory, which is bedeviled by conflicting aims and doctrines. It is true that men of letters were at that time more cognizant of critical authority than they have ever been since and much given to recommending their productions to the public as models of critical orthodoxy. Yet *All for Love, The Way of the World, The Rape of the Lock,* or *Tom Jones,* considered as aesthetic apprehensions of reality, often strike a modern reader as so many examples of the triumph of artistic instinct over inept theory. The requirement of probability and the stress on the didactic both obviously affect the relationship of literature to life; yet the two are incompatible, one tending toward fidelity to experience, the other toward some such patterning of events as that demanded by the notion of poetic justice. The norm of probability itself, though doubtless salutary in some respects, was responsible for a good deal of banal commentary and some that it is only charitable to label quaint. Fairies, Johns Hughes remarks in his edition of *The Faerie Queene* (1715), are not in themselves improbable, but Spenser's are because they are man-size.

The worst effect of this criterion on literary theory lay in fostering a constant confusion of art and life. How, asked the more intractable exponents of the dramatic unity of time, can two hours on stage represent two months? By the rule of probability John Dennis condemned the Greek tragic chorus as an absurdity; so, with less excuse, did that learned lover of Greek literature Thomas Gray, who in 1751 asked his friend Mason how Macbeth could have planned his murder or Hamlet upbraided his mother in the presence of "a gaping, singing, dancing, moralising, uninteresting crowd." The belief that truth was the basis of wit also contributed to a general distaste for allegory, or what Joseph Spence in

An Essay on Pope's Odyssey (1726) called "that absurdity of mixing fable and reality together," of which
Dryden's *Hind and Panther,* he thought, provided an
especially gross example. Years later, in *The Lives of the
English Poets,* Dr. Johnson was to make the same objection to Dryden's theology-talking beasts.

Yet though they often misconceived the essentially
formal functions of the ancient chorus and of allegory,
neoclassical writers had conventions aplenty of their
own to prevent the idea of imitating nature and the
stress on verisimilitude from generating a theory or practice of literary naturalism. The respect for the formal
exactions of genre and the related doctrine of following
classical models were sufficient of themselves to assure
an irreducible degree of aesthetic distance. Moreover, a
poem was looked on primarily as an artifact rather than
as an utterance by the poet, least of all as his confessional.
Romantic expressionism is a vulgar derivative of the
tradition of the poet as inspired visionary (*vates*), and
though this tradition was not without adherents in the
later eighteenth century it is the alternative conception
of the poet as craftsman (*poeta*) which predominates in
neoclassical poetics. On the eve of the Restoration
Abraham Cowley expressed the typical attitude when he
reminded his readers that the love lyrics in his volume of
Poems (1656) did not prove him amorous. "It is not in
this sense," he observed in the preface, "that *Poesie* is
said to be a kind of painting; it is not the *Picture* of the
Poet, but of things and persons imagined by him."

But if for at least a century after Cowley wrote few
people needed his warning against what is now called
the personal heresy, even fewer would have questioned
his reference to poetry as a kind of painting. Endowed
with a breadth of meaning entirely unjustified by its
restricting context in the *Epistle to the Pisos,* Horace's
phrase *ut pictura poesis* ("poetry is like painting") was
endlessly invoked to support an indiscriminate parallel
between what were called "the sister arts." Simonides'

figurative descriptions of poetry as a speaking picture and painting as dumb poetry lent added classical countenance to a facile ontological assimilation of the two major imitative arts that was on the whole unfortunate in its consequences. Robert Wolseley declared poetry and painting to be more alike than any other two things in existence, and then proceeded to defend the Earl of Rochester's bawdy verses by the precedent of several nudes by Titian, Raphael, and Michelangelo. Not all critics were quite so silly in the uses they made of the comparison, but even the best of them—Dryden, Dennis, Pope, Addison, Joseph Warton, and Hurd among lesser figures—subscribed to it in one form or another.

None of them seems to have noticed the inevitable confusions that must ensue from pressing the parallel, in disregard of profound differences, between a spatial and a temporal art. That service was finally performed by the German critic G. E. Lessing in his *Laokoon* (1766). The Abbé Dubos, whose treatise on the two arts was widely admired in England, had seen the impossibility of representing duration in painting, and now and then an English critic pointed to some less significant difference, or supposed difference, between the two media. In an essay on the *Parallel of Poetry and Painting* prefatory to his translation of du Fresnoy's *De arte graphica*, Dryden in 1695 concluded that poetry afforded more instruction, painting more delight. Richard Hurd thought it worthwhile mentioning that painting had some advantage in imitating the visible! In *The Loves of the Plants* (1789), Erasmus Darwin more pertinently noted that personifications and allegorical figures, effective in poetry, become improbable when visually presented. This line of thought approximates Lessing's, but Darwin does not develop it nor does he make any reference to the *Laokoon*.

It should of course be remembered that painting during this time was heavily moral and literary, its subjects drawn from the Bible, from ancient and modern literary classics, and from history. Unless this fact is kept in mind Joseph Warton may seem remarkably naive in his praise for the Count de Caylus' *Tableaux tirés de l'Iliade, et de l'Odyssée d'Homère* (1757), in which the author signalized what he took to be some unusually graphic passages in the epics. Warton shared the count's wonder that no artist had translated these scenes to canvas, since he would have only "to substitute his colours for the words of Homer." Unfortunately, less than a decade later Lessing attacked Caylus' book as a prime example of the loose thinking indulged by exponents of *ut pictura poesis*.

In keeping with this fondness for thinking of poetry as verbal pictures, and perhaps in some measure its result, is the predominantly visual conception of the imagination which appears for example in Addison's *Spectator* papers on the Pleasures of the Imagination and persists during much of the eighteenth century. Poetry's affinity with music, though much explored, seemed more remote, music being (despite Aristotle's assurance) less obviously imitative than the graphic arts. Like poetry, music had power to express emotions, but since it could not articulate them with verbal precision many writers concluded that music could have only a secondary, ancillary role when the two arts were combined in song. The contrasting romantic doctrine, best known in Poe and Pater, that music is the artistic ideal to which poetry aspires, is entirely foreign to the neoclassical spirit. The poet, Darwin remarked, "writes principally to the eye." Some writers even detected a perfect correspondence of genres between the sister arts, heroic and tragic poetry, as Dennis observed in *A Large Account of Taste in Poetry* (1702), answering to historical painting, comedy to portrait. In one of his dissertations, *Poetry Considered as an Imitative Art*, Thomas Twining pointed out that the verbal imitation of visible objects was the kind of imitation most people had in mind. "We say the poet has painted his object; we talk of imagery, of the lively colors of his description, and the masterly touches of his pencil."

Descriptive poetry, mainly of natural scenery, he adds, is a modern development unknown among the ancients, who "had no Thomsons, because they had no Claudes." His point was well taken, since perhaps the most valuable literary result of the *ut pictura poesis* obsession was the encouragement of that poetry of natural description in which the eighteenth century excelled. Thomson in his *Seasons* (1726–1730), like Pope in *Windsor Forest* (1713) and many others who followed them, consciously aimed at a kind of verbal landscape painting, and it is quite apparent that what many descriptive poets were "imitating" was not some real scene but a typical painting of one. A fair example of what was meant by "speaking picture" appears in Dryden's ode *To Mrs. Anne Killigrew, Excellent in the Two Sister-Arts of Poesie, and Painting* (1686). The lines illustrative of the "happy draught" of Anne's "pencil," beginning

> The Sylvan Scenes of Herds and Flocks
> And fruitful Plains and barren Rocks

immediately remind a reader of one of Nicolas Poussin's idyllic landscapes. Joseph Warton compared the wild romantic "scenes" in Thomson's *Seasons* to those of the landscapist Salvator Rosa. Sometimes this imitative process was reversed. Alexander Knox tells of an artist making a print of the poetic sketch of the woodman going forth at dawn in William Cowper's *The Task* (1785).

The ideal of verisimilitude was challenged by the growing taste for the Gothic mode that arose in the later eighteenth century. In 1765 Richard Hurd put truth of representation second to liveliness and defended the poet's right to deal with the incredible ("I had almost said the impossible . . ."). In his influential *Letters on Chivalry and Romance* (1762) he distinguished between philosophical truth and poetical truth and argued boldly for imaginative freedom. Hurd's aim, however, was only to establish some critical ground for the new taste for supernatural and magical elements in literature. Aes-

thetically speaking, his romanticism is hardly more satisfactory than the realism of Gray's rejection of the tragic
chorus. That verisimilitude in art is necessarily limited
by the demands of form and technique is a concept only
rarely and obscurely glimpsed at this time. Some writers
did sense the aesthetic poverty of a mere transcript of
reality. Amid the chorus of voices demanding truth in
poetry, it is refreshing to read in William Congreve's
letter to Dennis *Concerning Humour in Comedy* (1695)
that "if a Poet should steal a Dialogue of any length from
the *Ex-tempore* Discourse of the two Wittiest Men upon
Earth, he would find the Scene but coldly receiv'd by the
Town." (John Dryden's grasp of this truth will be treated
in the next chapter.) To note the fact, however, is not to
provide its theoretical justification, something neoclassical
thought never quite achieved. Addison, for example, is
well aware that a work of art takes on a value not found
in the reality it imitates, observing in *Spectator* 416 that
a verbal depiction of something is often more lively than
the thing itself. But his explanation is merely that the poet
reveals more of its aspects than a physical view takes in.
Why does the disagreeable (he instances a dunghill)
please when imitated? In *Spectator* 418 he ascribes this
effect to the reason rather than the imagination: we admire the aptness of the representation by comparing it
with our memory of the original. If it is something painful or terrible, as in tragedy, the pleasure is produced by
our awareness that we are not actually in danger, whereas
the sight of real suffering fails to delight because "the
object presses too close upon our senses." The inadequacy
of this account, which was echoed by others, was exposed
in David Hume's essay *Of Tragedy* (1757). Hume prefers the idea first advanced by the Abbé Dubos, who perceived that pleasure is caused by any arousal of the mind
from a state of torpor and listlessness. Since, however, this
response would be even greater at the sight of real pain,
Hume's conclusion is that the pleasure lies in the imitation itself, in "the very eloquence with which the melan-

choly scene is represented." In saying this, he apparently had some inkling that the aesthetic emotion is of a different order from the life emotion, that "tragedy is an imitation, and imitation is of itself always agreeable."

In general neoclassical usage, the term "probability" simply translates the French *vraisemblance,* designating conformity to what is commonly experienced or generally believed. There is hardly a hint of its Aristotelian sense of consistency with the norms and data of the fictive world of the poem. Something approaching this sense appears in the papers Addison devoted to an analysis of *Paradise Lost,* when he defends as probable the marvelous incident of the hellish spirits shrinking in stature, since the reader has been previously apprised of their power to do so. Similarly, the miraculous transformation of Odysseus' ship into a rock is not improbable because Homer makes it clear that it was done by the gods. Henry Fielding, in his chapter on the marvelous in *Tom Jones,* condemned the improbability of unmotivated last-act moral reformations of characters, but more because such behavior is incredible than because it violates the internal consistency of the play.

What finally permitted a sounder idea of artistic imitation was the new psychology which was gradually developed from the empiricism of Locke. Its most important result for literary criticism lay in turning attention from the work to the mind of the reader or audience, which in turn led to an increasingly articulate distinction between the imaginative and the rational faculties. As the apparent agency of the imagination in both creation and appreciation became clear, critics more and more perceived the limitations of the rationalist aesthetic of rules. Somewhat paradoxically, they began to grasp the necessary distortion imposed upon reality by mimesis when they abandoned the ambitious attempt to formulate a complete definition of imitation and turned instead to inquire "what it is natural for the imagination to be delighted with," as Sir Joshua Reynolds phrased it in the brilliant

thirteenth of the fifteen presidential *Discourses on Art*
he delivered to students at the Royal Academy between
1769 and 1790. Sir Joshua declared in a passage linking
eighteenth-century criticism to the *Biographia Literaria,*
that poetry

> sets out with a language in the highest degree artificial,
> a construction of measured words, such as never is, nor
> never was used by man. Let this measure be what it
> may, whether hexameter or any other metre used in
> Latin or Greek—or rhyme, or blank verse varied with
> pauses and accents, in modern languages,—they are all
> equally removed from nature, and equally a violation of
> common speech. When this artificial mode has been
> established as the vehicle of sentiment, there is another
> principle in the human mind, to which the work must
> be referred, which still renders it more artificial, carries
> it still further from common nature, and deviates only
> to render it more perfect. That principle is the sense of
> congruity, coherence, and consistency, which is a real
> existing principle in man; and it must be gratified.

But the *Discourse* should be studied in its entirety as the
apogee of neoclassical mimetic theory.

THE RULES

No aspect of the neoclassical aesthetic has received more attention than its emphasis upon prescriptive
rules for writing and judging literature; and certainly none
has been more widely deplored by critics and literary historians in subsequent periods. During the nineteenth century much of the allegedly inferior quality of neoclassical
poetry was charged against the insensate "rule mongering"
of the age in which it was written. Since then, modern
scholarship, abetted by a profound alteration in poetic
taste and critical attitude, has entered a more favorable
estimate of eighteenth-century literature which in turn
has made possible a more sympathetic examination of the
rationale of the critical rules.

This revisionism of modern opinion has not of course removed our suspicion that the very idea of explicit poetic rules implies a radical misconception of how poets write poetry and readers enjoy it. Nothing is therefore so reassuring to a modern student than to find that many eighteenth-century English writers themselves objected to the rules as often useless and sometimes prejudicial to good writing. Yet this fact has sometimes led to certain hasty conclusions that more considered scrutiny has rightly challenged: that the "best critics" of the age were simply opposed to the principle of rules; that the history of neoclassical criticism can be read as a gradual progress toward abandoning the principle entirely; and that the literature produced by neoclassical creative writers can be evaluated in terms of their relative success in struggling against it. Since this last conclusion is no more than peripheral to the subject of this book, I shall only remark in passing that those who maintain it take upon themselves the considerable burden of explaining how and why an age of such brilliant artistic achievement as the European Enlightenment was also an age centrally defective in its theory of art. The first conclusion can be shown to be essentially false and the second at best a distortion of the facts.

To maintain, to the contrary, that the leading critics of the time freely subscribed to the idea of literary regularity and that a good deal can be said to justify them in this, is not to deny that they often attacked certain specific rules or that they sometimes differed considerably in their opinions as to the efficacy of the rules in general. And certainly it would be frivolous to suggest that the principle of regularity did not spawn the kind of thing that deserves to be called rule mongering. Men like Dryden and Addison had reason enough for their references to "mechanical" rules and their sneers at "rigid" critics. In this connection it is customary to think especially of the excesses of Thomas Rymer's attack on Shakespeare, or of Jeremy Collier, who insisted (as Rymer in fact did not) on the strictest interpretation of the dramatic unities of time and place. It is more likely, I think, that Dryden and Addison had in mind certain Continental critics, whose obsession with prescriptive maxims carried them to extremes of pedantic nonsense never perpetrated on the other side of the Channel. The sixteenth-century Italian critic Francesco Robortelli argued for limiting stage time to a twelve-hour day, since men don't do anything at night, to which Alessandro Piccolomini later added that this could hold only for the temperate zone, where daylight does in fact last twelve hours. In his *Pratique du théâtre* (1657), the Abbé d' Aubignac solemnly reaffirmed Robortello's opinion. In the eighteenth century, France was still no freer of this kind of logic chopping than she had been earlier. Pierre Moreau cites one Buffier, who in 1728 actually prescribed a separate set of rules for each act of a play; and one Gaullyer, who in the same year collected and arranged over three hundred pages of imperatives for the dramatic poem.[1]

For reasons mentioned in the last chapter, advocacy of the rules and protests against them appear together in England from the Restoration onward, not infrequently in the writings of a single critic. Early and late in Dryden's criticism, for example, can be found both scrupulous obeisance to the dramatic unities and casual dismissal of them, depending on where one looks. In 1670 he prided himself on the care he had taken to observe the *liaison des scènes* and the laws of time and place in *Tyrranic Love;* eight years later, on the occasion of *All for Love,* he expressed his preference for the laws of his own country and his impatience with French regularity. A year later still, having in the meantime read Rymer's *Tragedies of the Last Age* (1678), he reversed ground again. In *The Grounds of Criticism in Tragedy* he argued virtually the whole case for dramatic regularity, regretting the double plot of his comedy *Marriage a-la-Mode,* censuring the disunity of Shakespeare's history plays and the "bombast" of his style, and capping the whole with a quotation from René Rapin in defense of the rules. This vacillation of opinion can in some small part be put down to lack of candor, but what it mainly reflects is deep-seated uncertainty. Dryden after all, like many others in England, combined an assurance that literature was regular with recurrent doubts that its laws had yet been fully discovered or that they were in every respect subject to neat codification. In the meantime he was apparently willing to explore alternate possibilities, knowing, as he says in the preface to *Sylvae* (1685), that critical precepts are like some mathematical demonstrations, "very specious in the diagram, but failing in the mechanic operation."

What needs chiefly to be noticed, however, is that not even those who most openly scorned the rules believed poetry to be a matter of lawless fancy. The comic playwright George Farquhar's *Discourse upon Comedy* (1702) is often cited as an example of total rebellion against the critical rules. Yet he insisted upon at least unity of plot as indispensable to the success of a play and is so far from any kind of romantic lawlessness as to declare judgment essential to literary composition. In 1724 Leonard Welsted's *Dissertation Concerning the Perfection of the English Language* sarcastically dismissed the entire canon of literary rules both ancient and modern as a useless set of obvious directives that "never made a good poet nor mended a bad one." Poetry, he was convinced, was a matter of innate taste, not of acquired laws. But even Welsted denied that poetry was irrational, and his iconoclasm did not prevent him from laying down three general rules for poetry, one of which can in fact be found in Horace's *Epistle to the Pisos*. Welsted's disgust with critical prescription doubtless owes something to Longinus' *On the Sublime*, which he had translated a dozen years earlier. From the appearance of Boileau's French version in 1674, this fragmentary Greek treatise of unknown date and uncertain authorship variously influenced English criticism. The part played by its stress on "transport" over persuasion, and on innate talent over acquired craft, in qualifying and finally discrediting rationalist theory is undeniable though difficult to isolate from other forces tending to the same end. Addison, who in Professor Samuel H. Monk's judgment[2] did more than any other Englishman to spread the vogue of Longinus, defined the sublime as that effect produced in art by deviating from the rules. And Longinus' name was sometimes, as by John Husbands in 1731, coupled with the notion of *je ne sais quoi,* or the "grace beyond the reach of art." Yet it would be incorrect to equate Longinianism with opposition to the principle of rules. The author of *On the Sublime* does prefer a work of faulty genius to one of regular and faultless mediocrity, which may have inspired Addison's notion of what constituted sublimity. But the very *raison d'être* of Longinus' treatise is his express conviction that the sublime itself is subject to laws that can be known and formulated. It is therefore no anomaly that the greatest English Longinian of them all, John Dennis, insisted throughout his entire career on the necessity of knowing and following the poetic rules.

The still common impression that English criticism during the eighteenth century entailed a progressive turning away from the rules and a rejection of the concept of regular art is hardly borne out by the facts. Objections to this or that rule continue to be made, but with no discernible weakening of the conviction that literature like all art was governed by certain essential laws whose discovery and propagation were, as Dr. Johnson thought, part of the critic's proper business. Although he too regarded the bulk of the received poetic canons as so many arbitrary edicts that no poet was obliged to honor, he believed that a few were, in the words of *Rambler* 156, "invincibly supported by their conformity to the order of nature and operations of the intellect." The difference now is that few any longer believed as Dennis, Shaftesbury, and Gildon had done, that the poor quality of modern poetry resulted exclusively from the poets' disregard of the principles of their craft. It is that earlier simplistic concept of the creative process that Joseph Warton had in mind in his ode *To Fancy* (1746), in which he called for some new poet to

> *win applause*
> *Beyond cold critic's studied laws.*

Rebel against many of the critical assumptions of the great Augustans, downgrader of Pope, chief spokesman for a new dispensation in literary taste, Warton nonetheless listed the dramatic unities of time and place among several rules validated by nature and necessity. He thought of Aristotle's *Poetics* as an indispensable critical Euclid, criticized Nicholas Rowe's *Jane Shore* for violating the unity of time, and even regretted that Addison had not made dramatic time in *Cato* exactly equal to time of representation. These opinions from the first volume of the *Essay on the Genius and Writings of Pope* (1756) had not altered by 1782, the date of the second volume, in which he warmly admires the French dramatists for their strict observance of the unities. More typically post-Augustan are the attitudes of David Hume and Sir Joshua Reynolds. Both denied the efficacy of a conscious application of abstract laws in creation or criticism, while insisting that poetry must nonetheless be confined by rules. According to Hume in his *On the Standard of Taste* (1757), these are apprehended by the poet either intuitively or by observation; more Longinian, Sir Joshua, as in *Idler* 76 (1759), removed genius entirely from the province of rules.

What does become increasingly frequent after 1750 is critical relativism, which rejects not the principle of aesthetic order itself but the notion of a single and universally valid classical system. This is implied in many of the defenses of Shakespeare and Spenser, coming to its fullest expression in Hurd's *Letters on Chivalry and Ro-*

mance and the second edition (1762) of Thomas Warton's *Observations on the Faerie Queene*. Yet even the
historical relativism of these men represents less a basic
change in aesthetic theory than an effective critical justification of an altered poetic taste,[3] since protests against
judging every kind of literature by the square of Greece
and Rome had been a familiar motif in English criticism
since Elizabethan times.

The requirements that he imitate nature and that he
conform to the rules did not present the poet with either
a free choice or a dilemma. Whichever of these aims he
took as his guide, he was in theory also fulfilling the
other, since the rules were no more than a codification of
the order manifested in nature. The passage from Rapin
with which Dryden concluded his *Grounds of Criticism*
justifies the rules as the reduction of nature into method,
a definition repeated by Rymer, Dennis, and others. This
conception was not merely a strategic dodge to found
classical regularity on something more enduring than the
ipse dixit of ancient pronouncement. It expressed the
genuine faith that art necessarily partook of and reflected
that harmony and order which reason discovered throughout the universe.

This ultimate equation of mimesis and composition by
rule is also the first step toward understanding why even
the most original thinkers of the day were so long pre-
occupied with the rules in the face of all that could be
said against them. The respect for authority that had suf-
ficed to validate the literary doctrines of an Aristotle or
a Horace during the Renaissance had been largely eroded
by the new philosophy of the seventeenth century. If despite this changed attitude toward the past the classical
literary lawgivers still seemed worth serious attention, it
was because it could be plausibly argued that their precepts were not so many *a priori* declarations but rather
conclusions reached by the very process of inductive reasoning which modern philosophers exalted as the one sure

road to truth. Thus Pope's *An Essay on Criticism* affirmed that

> *Those rules of old* discovered, not devised,
> Are Nature still, but Nature methodized.

This line of reasoning further explains why the classical literary system was so largely and so long exempt from the general discrediting of ancient learning effected by modern scientific discoveries. The fact seemed puzzling to a few writers at the time, just as it has been misinterpreted by others since. At an early stage of his undistinguished career, Charles Gildon asked why Greek poetics should still be held in esteem when Greek physics and medicine were exploded; and until quite recently some scholars were arguing that the neoclassical respect for classical rules was antithetical to the spirit of neoclassical science.[4] It is because the opposite of this thesis is true that the declining prestige of the classical rules-based poetics was actually restored by the triumph of philosophical rationalism. In the light of this realization we have to reject the view that in their serious commitment to Aristotelian teaching Augustan men of letters were in perverse reaction against the intellectual currents of the time. Some hint of a sounder explanation is provided by their reiteration of that word *method*. From its inception in the writings of Bacon the new science had taught that sound progress in any branch of learning depended on the adoption of a correct method. Descartes launched his philosophic revolution by writing a *Discourse on Method*. The method of any science was embodied in a set of rules, principles, or axioms that were so many means to an end. Of course these means had to be the correct ones. But whereas modern investigators had shown those of the ancient natural scientists to be in many cases false, no modern had been able to demonstrate with any finality a similar deficiency in the poetics of Aristotle, Horace, Longinus, or Quintilian. The undiminished beauty and power of the Greek and Latin masterpieces from which the literary methods of these critics were derived were themselves strong presumptive evidence to the contrary.

Presumptive but not necessarily conclusive. The opinion of many is fairly summed up in Pope's praise of the ancient rules as "just precepts . . . from great examples given." This is the essence of Rymer's view. Others were not so sure. Dennis was no less convinced than Rymer that "there are proper Means for the attaining of every End, and those Means in Poetry we call the Rules," as he wrote in *The Grounds of Criticism in Poetry* (1704). Yet he felt that some of the classical rules were relevant only in a pagan culture, and his most ambitious theorizing was devoted to the discovery and elaboration of a new poetics sounder and more universal than the old. With no disrespect for Aristotle's inductive skill, a modern critic could claim the advantage of a larger and more varied body of literature on which to exercise his own. In the *Heads of an Answer to Rymer* Dryden wondered whether Aristotle himself might not have altered his conception of tragic catharsis if he had seen English tragedies. How far Greco-Roman literary theory could be regarded as final or complete, a question crucial to the quarrel between the "Moderns" and the "Ancients," was constantly debated. But spokesmen for both sides in the controversy assumed the possibility of some workable set of rules as means to the end of creating literature; and they were likely to be among those best read in contemporary philosophy and most convinced of its general utility.

As the eighteenth century progressed certain psychologically oriented theories, evolved from Locke's empiricism and exalting the imagination at the expense of the reason, threw increasing doubt on the aesthetic sufficiency of the Cartesian epistemology. It is no accident that this development was attended by the final vindication of those who, innocent of philosophy, had all along doubted that a poem could be written to prescription. But neither the enlargement of the imagination's part in the creative act nor the substitution of rule-transcending genius for the conscious application of rules in any way weakened the belief in orderly art. In *An Essay on Genius* (1774), Alexander Gerard, one of a host of Scottish writers who made verbose contributions to aesthetics during the second half of the century, distinguished true imagination from the sort of disorderly fancy which, he said, had produced *The Faerie Queene*. Endowed with true imagination, genius had no need of rules; Homer's genius is as *regular* as it is vast.

The qualities of harmony, symmetry, and order in a work of art—the mutual accommodation of parts to whole and means to end—suffered no devaluation when critics stopped talking about the rules and turned instead to an analysis of the imagination. One modern aesthetician has recently found it startling that in the *Essays on the Nature and Principles of Taste* (1790) Archibald Alison, after adopting an empirical basis for criticism, condemned Shakespeare's tragi-comedy as severely "as could be wished by the most rigorous neoclassicist."[5] But there is no need to be startled. Alison's position only reminds us that neither the replacement of rationalism by empiricism nor the decline of prescriptive rule mongering logically entailed an abandonment of specific rules or of regularity. For if the rules were nature methodized, the imagination, as Gerard pointed out, was the "methodizing power."

THE CREATIVE PROCESS AND THE POETIC FUNCTION

Though the earliest neoclassicists believed that the conscious application of the rules could assure successful composition, none of them supposed this possible without natural talent. In the roles assigned by their poetics to fancy and judgment, nature and art, taste and learning (overlapping terms), the first of each pair is clearly given the greater importance. However, this fact is easily obscured by the emphasis placed in critical dis-

cussion on judgment, art, and the deliberate application
of rule; but this was both because the other requisite of
natural genius was taken for granted and because it was
regarded as a potentially dangerous faculty. The philosopher Hobbes is rightly given a large share of the credit,
or blame, for this peculiar preoccupation of neoclassical
creative theory with deliberate craftsmanship. That the
poet's reason should govern his fancy and restrain its
excesses is a constant theme in the aesthetics of the great
mechanist. Yet not even Hobbes assigned judgment other
than a secondary though indispensable part in the total
creative process; and in his *History of English Poetry*
Thomas Warton could quote the *Leviathan* to the effect
that in a poem the fancy must predominate.

Nonetheless, in the first decades after the Restoration
so great was the fear of the unbridled fancy as the source
of all that was disorderly and enthusiastic that moral, psychological, and critical speculation is heavy with warnings against it and with tiresome reminders of how
essential it is that the activities of all men, including authors, be guided by their rational faculties. The net result was so far to discredit the extrarational elements in
artistic creation that much of the critical effort of the
final years of the eighteenth century went into a com-
pensatory rehabilitation of the imagination, as by then it
was generally named. For Dryden in 1664 fancy (or wit
in one of its myriad senses) was a "high-ranging spaniel"
needing control, an image taken up by the redoubtable
Rymer, who in *Tragedies of the Last Age* is characteristically graphic: "*Fancy* leaps, and frisks, and away she's
gone; whilst *reason* rattles the chains, and follows after."
Or, as Dryden had it in *The Grounds of Criticism in
Tragedy*, it is "a hot-mouthed jade without a curb,"
which Pope later dignified to Pegasus, who

like a generous horse,
Shows most true mettle when you check his course.

At worst, unrestrained fancy was, or led to, madness, as the Earl of Mulgrave sang in his verse *Essay upon Poetry* (1682); and Thomas Shadwell went so far as to declare madmen simply more fanciful than anyone else. Even critics who entertained a more creditable conception of the inventive powers were nonetheless convinced that genius unaided by judgment, which usually meant the rules, could produce nothing of value.

Entirely consistent with this rationalistic view of literary composition was the high value placed on the painstaking revision and polishing of one's work. In fact this labor of the file, as Horace calls it, was one of the chief modes of the judgment's operation. It was the second half of a two-step sequence, reason "correcting" and ordering what fancy had "found," in a procedure opening a split of form and content not healed for a century thereafter. Whatever its theoretical deficiencies, however, it was appropriate to an age whose literary men took pride in meticulous workmanship. Everyone recalls Pope's dissatisfaction with any of his lines not given the last corrective touch of grace and precision. Addison, Joseph Warton reports, used to stop the presses to add a preposition or conjunction to a *Spectator* essay. This attitude toward literary composition explains what would otherwise be a puzzlingly honorific use of the words *laborious* and *labored* in the criticism of this time. Today we always damn a book by calling it labored, but Addison's characterization of Virgil's third *Georgic* as "the most labored of them all" was intended as praise. Nor was there any danger of its being taken otherwise at a time when poets respected Boileau's injunction to bring their work twenty times back to the loom. They expected little from anything dashed off in a rapture of "inspiration" (a word which Davenant had called dangerous) and thereafter never retouched.

None of the foregoing should be taken to mean that neoclassical writers relished what we now mean by a labored style. In the Prologue to *The Way of the World* Congreve confessed that he had wrought his scenes with toil but asked no indulgence from the audience on that account if the result was dullness. What was most admired was a mean between the rhapsodic and the plodding. The proper labor of art had to be concealed; facility and ease, not visible effort, were the effects to be aimed at. But these qualities were seen to depend more on deliberate workmanship than is usually thought today.

> *True ease in writing comes from art not chance.*

Joseph Warton's comment on Pope's familiar line is representative. The works of La Fontaine and others like him, he observed, "cost them much pains, and were labored into that facility for which they are so famous"; and Molière spent days searching for a proper epithet or an apt rhyme, though what he finally produced has "all the flow and freedom of conversation." When Spence remarked on the many corrections and alterations in Pope's draft copy of the *Iliad* translation, the poet assured him that "those parts which have been the most corrected read the easiest."

During and after the romantic period there was little sympathy for this appreciation of conscious artistry. In the nineteenth century most people (Poe is an interesting exception) felt quite certain that the inevitable result of deliberate contrivance in the writing of a poem would be to experience a contrived effect in the reading of it. This belief is no longer so strong as it once was. In the aftermath of T. S. Eliot's cogent argument, in explicit rebuttal of Matthew Arnold, that "the labour of sifting, combining, constructing, expunging, correcting, testing," comprises the larger part of creation, we have come to treat this aspect of the neoclassical view of literary creation with renewed respect. There is, however, another principle which modern theorists hesitate to confirm and some vehemently oppose. In his *Traité du poème épique* (1675), Boileau's friend René Le Bossu held that the epic

poet must begin his work by first choosing the moral lesson he wishes to inculcate and then finding an illustrative plot and characters, as, he maintained, Homer had
done. Le Bossu was thus restating the traditional account of how to write an epic poem which English
Restoration critics following him adopted and extended
to other genres as well. Dryden reported having employed
this method in writing his tragedy *The Conquest of
Granada* and advocated it again in the *Parallel of Poetry
and Painting*. Addison, however, disagreed. Although he
too thought some instructive moral to be the basis of an
epic poem, when he came to write his *Spectator* papers
on *Paradise Lost* he expressed doubt that the poet first
decided on his moral and *then* invented a fable to suit.
Dr. Johnson thought Milton had done exactly that, but,
for all his moralism, doubted that any other epic poet had
ever composed according to Le Bossu's prescription. Despite Addison's dissent, the French theorist's belief in the
priority of idea to image in the creative process prevailed
throughout the century in England. The poets themselves
often testified in its favor. According to Spence's *Anecdotes,* Pope said of *An Essay on Criticism* that he had
"digested all the matter, in prose, before turning it into
verse." Even in the last decade, though the heart had
largely replaced the head as the source of "true" poetry,
Alexander Knox, reviewing Cowper's poems, approvingly
translated Horace's *Verbaque provisam rem non invita
sequentur* as "apt words spontaneously follow just conceptions." Knox's wording ("spontaneously") is less bla-
tantly disruptive of form and content than the formula-
tions of earlier writers. Yet like them and like the dualism
of fancy and judgment, it assumes that poetry is simply
thought decorated by the superadded graces of fine diction, imagery, rhythm, and so forth, whereas modern
poetics postulates instead an organic structure in which
idea has no being apart from its sensuous embodiment in
these formal elements. One current school of theorists
has in effect actually reversed Le Bossu's creative proce-

dure. They point to several modern poets, Eliot and Valéry among them, who have testified that their poems begin not with an abstract theme but with only a rhythmic beat or an image detached from any concept. The meaning of the poem (content) is not in any conscious sense known beforehand, but rather "discovered" in the act of composition. Or, as it has been alternately stated, the poet "thinks in images."

This total reversal of the preromantic psychology of poetic creation is doubtless open to the charge of oversimplifying the elusively complex interaction between the intellectual and the sensuous that takes place in the mind of a poet as he writes. In its way no less reductive than the neoclassical conception, it is perhaps preferable only because more consonant with what we know—or think we know—about the unique amalgamation of form and matter in the poetic symbol as the essential constituent of a poem. Since not even this much would be granted by some contemporary theorists, it seems hardly profitable to attempt to arbitrate between rival theories here. We need only remark that this particular issue reveals how a general conception of the nature of literature can be an obstacle to the satisfactory solution of specific problems. John Dennis was perceptive enough to glimpse the interdependency of content and technique. In his *Grounds of Criticism in Poetry* he argued impressively that religion is the basis of the greatest poetry because religion occasions the strongest passions. Passion in turn necessarily gives rise to harmony and figurative language; poetry is thus a passionate utterance. His reasoning led him to a near anticipation of Coleridge's insight that the poetic imagination reveals itself in "a more than usual state of emotion, with more than usual order." But the opposites that Coleridge was able to reconcile in the *Biographia Literaria* merely puzzle Dennis. He finds it "a little odd to consider that passion, which disturbs the soul, should occasion it to produce harmony, which seems to imply the order and composure of it. . . ." Dennis' theoretical helplessness in the face of the truth he has so unerringly grasped about poetry measures the limitations of the critical rationalism to which his age was committed.

For all this, the account of the creative process advanced during this period squared well enough with what writers then conceived to be the purpose and value of a literary work. As with the doctrine of imitating nature, neoclassical literary thought here continued the Renaissance tradition, which had adopted Horace's double end of *utile dulce*. The poet must instruct and delight.

In general, pleasure was considered instrumental to the ultimate end of moral instruction. But the two aims were variously related and a few critics placed the stress on pleasure. Cowley called delight the "main end of Poesie," as did Dryden on at least one occasion. Some thought the function varied with the genre, the superiority of epic and tragedy over lesser kinds consisting precisely in their greater power to impart profound truths. In *Tragedies of the Last Age*, Rymer put it most succinctly:

1. I believe the end of all Poetry is to *please*.
2. Some sorts of Poetry please without profiting.
3. I am confident that whoever writes a Tragedy cannot please but must also profit; 'tis the Physic of the mind that he makes palatable.

The rationale of Rymer's confidence that a pleasurable tragedy must be morally sound is worth examination. The pleasure that a tragedy affords consists in its being a mimetic demonstration of the operancy of law, of universal order, in the loftiest affairs of men. It is pleasurable because of its beauty, but this beauty comes ultimately from perceiving the harmony of that nature which the tragedy imitates. A universal order, when it is manifested in human action, must be a moral order implying both the possibility of willful violation and the justice of retribution. For this reason Rymer gives poetic justice a central position in his theory of tragedy. Any play in which villainy goes unpunished or injured virtue finds no reward distorts the moral order, denies its beauty, and thus nullifies the pleasure of the beholder. On the same grounds it is morally vicious. When the tragic poet denies poetic justice, Dennis wrote in *The Advancement and Reformation of Modern Poetry* (1701), his play is "either an empty amusement, or a scandalous and pernicious Libel upon the Government of the World." It is by this same grand logic that the most uncompromising exponents of literature's moral end saw in it the most irrefutable argument for the rules. Foreshadowing Matthew Arnold's substitution of poetry for religion, Dennis assigned poets the lofty mission of restoring the pristine order violated by the Fall of man. But he could not imagine how they could achieve this high purpose if poetry itself was "irregular and extravagant." The rules, everyone agreed, were means to an end. In the eyes of critics who were most concerned that the end be edification, the irregular poet was not only artistically deficient; he stood convicted of vicious intent. It is no accident that Jeremy Collier, whose *Short View of the Immorality and Profaneness of the English Stage* (1698) charged the leading Restoration playwrights with bawdiness and irreligion, should also have been a strict advocate of stage decorum and the dramatic unities.

Readily justifiable by the logic of Rymer's and Dennis' assumptions, the rule of poetic justice, as they conceived it, nonetheless implies a remarkably shallow and restricted idea of literary morality. It embarrassed Dryden, who sensibly argues in the *Heads of an Answer to Rymer* that an audience could be trusted to disapprove of crime and vice in a play even if the plot did not show them punished. Likewise with virtue. The poet, Dryden felt, met his moral obligation simply by showing it "always amiable though . . . unfortunate." In *Spectator* 40 Addison, whose own tragic hero, Cato, earned only suicide by his virtues, was more peremptory. The rule of poetic justice is founded neither in nature nor in literature: the good suffer and the wicked triumph in life, and in the finest tragedies—he instances *Venice Preserved, All for Love,* and *Oedipus Rex*—the heroes meet with calamity. *King Lear,* he adds, lost half its beauty when Shakespeare's ending was replaced by one less shocking to our moral sense. Unconvinced, Dennis retorted that poetic justice was the very foundation of all the rules, and pitted his "logic" against Addison's appeal to experience: "For what Tragedy can there be without a Fable? or what Fable without a Moral? or what Moral without poetical Justice?"

In the last analysis, the neat congruence between didacticism and the basic premises of neoclassical literary theory suggests wherein that theory fell short. The many pronouncements about the poet's moral function and about his primary duty to instruct and edify his readers strike us today as blurring the distinction between literature and indoctrination to such an extent that the poet's role is demeaned to that of the propagandist. Literature, we are prepared to admit, above all the greatest literature, is fraught with values; it arises from urgencies of love or indignation or aspiration that can ultimately be referred to certain moral or intellectual categories of which it is an aesthetic embodiment, and it elicits a response radically conditioned by human values. The trouble with neoclassical literary didactic theory is that it typically distorted the relationship between the moral and the aesthetic. It prompted critics to ask the wrong questions and often to make statements that seem glaringly irrelevant. It is hard not to smile—or wince—when we find Lewis Theobald solemnly proclaiming at the end of a discussion of the plot of *King Lear*: "Hence arise two practical morals: the first, a caution against rash and unwary bounty; the second, against the base returns and ingratitude of children to an aged parent." Francis Gentleman was more at ease discussing Addison's *Cato,* where "instruction pours forth from every line. . . ."

"The *Odyssey,*" Pope wrote in a 1726 postscript to his

translation of it, "is a moral and political work, instructive to all degrees of men and filled with images, examples, and precepts of civil and domestic life." Hard to prove "false," Pope's observation seems nevertheless to miss the point. We are sure it has little to do with why we read Homer's epic, and we may even harbor the suspicion that Pope didn't read it for that reason either.

Why then did he say it? The answer lies not so much in any explicit aspect of the didactic principle itself as in certain ill-discriminated assumptions that helped to assure its general acceptance. The fact is, even if Pope's pleasure in reading the *Odyssey* was not directly produced by its political and moral precepts, we can be sure he would have thought less of the poem if he did not find them there. In his day, not only the epic but virtually all poetry was liable to be judged by the criterion of social utility broadly defined. If a poem or a prose work did not "adorn vertue and procure her lovers," as Hobbes had somewhat unfortunately phrased it, it had at least to inculcate some bit of wisdom or, as in the case of such "process" poems as William Somervile's *The Chace,* offer instruction in some practical activity. Even purely descriptive poems did not escape an injection of the sententious at some point or other. This conception of literary value is obviously suitable to the priority assigned to moral abstractions in the procedure a poet was supposed to follow in writing his poem. Le Bossu's creative theory is the creative theory of a fundamentally utilitarian aesthetic.

No one seemed to doubt that literature was for *use,* for teaching men how to live, or to suppose that any other value it might have could be sufficient justification for its existence. In claiming that "a system of civil and economical prudence" could be collected from Shakespeare's works, Dr. Johnson knew he was placing the English dramatist, with Homer, in the highest rank. Though Joseph Warton concluded that didactic poetry *per se* was inferior to other kinds, he still gave as his reason for preferring the *Odyssey* to the *Iliad* that its moral applied to a broader portion of society; it inculcated the duties of benevolence, charity, hospitality. That new genre, the novel, constantly recommended itself on didactic grounds. After duly cautioning readers against the pernicious effects of the older prose romances, James Beattie was glad to applaud Daniel Defoe's *Robinson Crusoe* for extolling the mechanic arts and communicating at once the virtues of society and of independence. Invented by and for the middle class, in whose mores the Puritanism of an earlier time had become a morality of prudence leading to commercial success, the novel upheld ideals humbler and more unabashedly utilitarian than the heroic qualities celebrated in aristocratic tragedy and epic. "I declare," Henry Fielding wrote to George Lyttleton in the Dedication to *Tom Jones,* "that to recommend goodness and virtue hath been my sincere endeavour in this history." What the book itself chiefly advocates (if a moral *must* be drawn from it) is an alteration of the smart-aleck crack "If you can't be good, be careful" to "If you *are* good, you'd best be careful"—a lesson it takes Tom eight hundred pages to get into his head. The significant point, however, is that Fielding felt constrained to profess a moral aim at all, not the accuracy, or even the sincerity, of the way he phrased it. Such professions were part of the strategy adopted by the pioneers of the novel to assure that the public would accord the new genre literary status. This could not be done by offering one's wares as mere entertainment, or even as having some more sophisticated kind of aesthetic value. Appeals of this kind meant little to readers habituated to thinking of a book as something having humanistic instrumental value. Defoe advertised his *Moll Flanders* more for its moral than its fable, and called attention to how scrupulously he had observed poetic justice, the immoral characters either punished or penitent at the end.

It seems highly unlikely that the worldly patrons of a Restoration comedy sought or received anything remotely like the sober preachments Samuel Richardson's readers

found in *Pamela* or *Clarissa Harlowe*. Yet George Farquhar traced the origin of comedy to Aesop's *Fables* and
defined it as "an agreeable vehicle for counsel and re-
proof. . . . *Utile dulci* . . . must be our business. . . ."
Other comic dramatists defended their plays against Jeremy Collier's charges of immorality in much the same
terms. In a *Vindication* of two of his most licentious plays,
The Relapse and *The Provok'd Wife,* Sir John Vanbrugh
argued that the comic poet's business was to teach people
to behave well by the spectacle of misconduct. The
sophistry of his reasoning suggests lip service to a norm
he dared not defy; he commands more respect for his protest against overt moralizing, against the presence of some
"Philosopher" on stage to spell out the lesson senten-
tiously. But it was Dennis who put the moral case for the
comedy of manners most convincingly in 1722. Years earlier, in *Spectator* 65, Sir Richard Steele had sought to
prepare the public taste for a favorable reception of the
new sentimental comedy best exemplified by his *The
Conscious Lovers* (1722). To this end he attacked Etherege's *Man of Mode,* one of the most popular and successful plays of the Restoration, for offering a pernicious
model of the fine gentleman. In his refutation Dennis
pointed to Aristotle, Horace, and Greek comic practice
in support of his argument that in order to teach against
vice, comedy must be "an Imitation of corrupt and de-
generate Nature"; it must ridicule, and only vice is ridiculous.

The long debate over the alleged immorality of the
stage that was initiated by Collier's diatribe is clouded by
motives of self-justification and personal animus (Dennis
and Steele were literary enemies). In the sense that the
new moralizing comedy of sentiment triumphed on the
stage and in critical opinion, Collier is generally thought
to have won the argument. What seems clear in retro-
spect is that his enemies the playwrights assured him the
victory in advance by attempting to defeat him on his
own grounds, when they might better have exposed the

inadequacy of his crude conception of literary morality. Here and there in their rebuttals hints of this sounder strategy do appear, but always subordinated to expressions of satirical defiance or counterarguments based on Collier's own moralistic premises. Their failure to adopt a better course, however, becomes understandable in light of the fact that those premises were fostered by a literary theory that authorized no dissent from Pope's belief that no writing was good unless it made for the betterment of humanity, or Dr. Johnson's that it was always a writer's duty to leave the world better than he found it.

III *JOHN DRYDEN*

John Dryden is easily the greatest English literary critic of the seventeenth century. This would be true even without the advantage of a prose style that at its best comes close to Bishop Thomas Sprat's ideal of "natural easiness and unaffected grace, where nothing seems to be studied, yet everything is extraordinary." It remains true even after taking full account of the several places in which his judgment is warped by animosity, patriotism, flattery, or momentary awe of Thomas Rymer. These faults, seldom grave, were more than offset by personal qualities of mind and temperament that superbly equipped Dryden for the critic's role. Besides a skeptical turn of mind that saved him from the dogmatism to which his order-seeking age was prone, he had an unusual flair for close reasoning. Above all, there was the sensitivity of his poetic genius. Most often Dryden the critic is Dryden the poet talking about his craft. With the notable exception of *An Essay of Dramatic Poesy* (1668), the bulk of his criticism is occasional, prefaces or epistles dedicatory to his printed plays, translations, and poetic miscellanies. Like much of T. S. Eliot's critical writings, most of Dryden's is accordingly the by-product of his poetic workshop, and his exploration of literary problems is enlivened by a practitioner's immediacy of

interest. Not only the abstract justification of this or that
principle of dramatic composition would engage Dryden's
attention, but whether and how far it might contribute
to the success of the plays he was writing at the moment
for courtly London audiences. At the same time he shared
his contemporaries' preoccupation with theoretical questions as such, and a great deal of his critical prose reveals
a high zest for intellectual speculation, a delicious curios-
ity to test all sides of controversial issues, to propose new
definitions and sift old formulas. "Strong reason predominated in his intellectual operations," and "the favorite exercise of his mind was ratiocination," as Dr. Johnson was
to observe.

Yet it would be anachronistic to imagine Dryden a
critic by turns academic and practical. He lived in a time
when writers were more respectful of critical theories and
theorists than they have ever been since. When he has
Crites, Eugenius, Lisideius, and Neander, the leisurely
debaters of *An Essay of Dramatic Poesy,* set forth the
relative merits of the ancient, modern, French, and English stages, it never occurs to him that he was not doing
something as useful to his success as an aspiring playwright as it was intellectually stimulating. If in reading
Dryden's critical essays we invariably feel the presence of
a living personality, it is because he so constantly seeks
to review the rule in the light of his creative experience
or, reciprocally, to "justify" what he has just been doing
by invoking some esteemed precedent or critical prescription. Sometimes this process degenerates into special
pleading, as when he points to Homer's Achilles and
Tasso's Rinaldo to excuse the spurious heroics of his own
Almanzor in *The Conquest of Granada* (1672). More
often though, it quietly deflates the pretentions of theory
itself. In the Preface to *All for Love* (1678), foreseeing
critical disapproval of the scene in which Octavia and
Cleopatra indulge in mutual invectives, he defends it by
remarking that "after all, though the one were a Roman
and the other a queen, they were both women." No one,

not Dr. Johnson himself, ever more effectively exposed the absurdity of Rymer's dehumanized conception of character decorum.

The chief subjects of Dryden's criticism are several. First in order of time and in bulk is the drama. Looking back over his career in 1693, he saw himself as a pioneer in dramatic criticism. When he began to write no living or past English master of it existed. Shakespeare had written "happily," not "knowingly or justly"; Ben Jonson had not passed on his critical knowledge. So, Dryden concludes, he had to set out on a vast ocean with only the Ancients as his polestar, the rules of the modern French stage being unsuitable to English taste. There is some exaggeration in this complaint, but not much. Although *An Essay of Dramatic Poesy* derives as much from ancient Greek and contemporary French theory as from Elizabethan example, it is in fact the first considerable treatise on the dramatic art in our language. Dryden's second interest was the epic, or heroic poem, the grand genre in which all his life he longed to distinguish himself and which, in any case, was closely associated in his mind with tragedy, the heroic play. On satire, the field of his greatest poetic achievement, he wrote less, and less memorably. The lengthy *Discourse Concerning the Original and Progress of Satire* (1693), though the product of a great satirist writing in a great age of satire, is a somewhat disappointing performance. He spends pages worrying the dry bones of learned speculation on the subject by Scaliger, Heinsius, Casaubon, and Dacier. In compensation, there follow some livelier pages on Horace, Juvenal, and Persius, treated by the "new method" of comparative criticism. Best and most revealing of all, as the opinion of so skilled a practitioner, is his statement that the satiric talent

> must be inborn; it must proceed from a genius, and particular way of thinking, which is not to be taught; and therefore not to be imitated by him who has it not from nature. How easy it is to call rogue and villain,

and that wittily! But how hard to make a man appear a fool, a blockhead, or a knave, without using any of those opprobrious terms!

Aptly descriptive of his own, and of Pope's, finest satiric "characters," this passage also deserves notice for its stress on genius, on what is inborn and "not to be taught" or imitated, terms that already challenge the predominant rationalism of this early phase of neoclassical thought.

Hardly less interesting than his ideas on these important literary kinds are his observations on the art of translation and on prosody. Here again his concern stems from the needs of his practice. What he has to say on prosody especially betrays an urgency arising from his ambition to complete the refinement of English numbers initiated by Waller and Denham. Like others at this time, he regretted the lack of any fixed system of English versification. In the Dedication to his translation of the *Aeneid* (1697), where the most extended discussion of verse technique occurs, he reported having long since compiled materials for an English *Prosodia*. But it was never published.

Deliberately rambling and informal, Dryden's essays are hard to arrange in any order of excellence. The best of them can stand pruning and the poorest are seldom without some redeeming distinction. But *An Essay of Dramatic Poesy,* written near the beginning of his career, and the *Preface to Fables Ancient and Modern* (1700), at the end of it, are justly admired above the rest. Organized as a dialogue, a form suited to his native skepticism, and devoted chiefly to the drama, the *Essay* in fact touches on almost every contemporary literary issue. Remarkably like it in style (considering the years separating them), the *Preface to Fables* is very different in tone. It is pervaded by the relaxed urbanity of a man secure in his fame, confident of his mastery, and beyond desire or hope of worldly favor. Having translated some favorite authors, Homer, Ovid, Boccaccio, Chaucer, he is in a mood to talk about them—and wonderful talk it is. "The matter and manner of their tales," he says of Chaucer's Canterbury Pilgrims,

> and of their telling, are so suited to their different educations, humours, and callings, that each of them would be improper in any other mouth. Even the grave and serious characters are distinguished by their several sorts of gravity: their discourses are such as belong to their age, their calling, and their breeding; such as are becoming of them, and of them only—

sentences that might stand as epigraph to a host of studies by modern analysts of the psychological precision of Chaucer's portraiture. It is some indication of Dryden's critical independence that he expressed such appreciative delight at all in 1700. Half a century later the learned Thomas Warton was still complaining in his *Observations* on Spenser of a lack of appreciation for Chaucer, whose poems continued to be regarded as "pieces better calculated to gratify the antiquarian than the critic."

The much longer *Essay of Dramatic Poesy* is also richer in significant material. The four disputants first agree on a definition of a play: *"A just and lively image of human nature, representing its passions and humours . . . for the delight and instruction of mankind."* This definition is obviously couched in terms favorable to the English drama, for which Dryden himself will speak in the person of Neander; but Crites and Lisideius, apologists respectively for the ancients and the modern French, make no objection. Speaking first, Crites lauds the classical poets, from whose dramatic masterpieces Aristotle and Horace derived the principles of the genre. Eugenius, after observing that poetry like everything else improves with time (a fallacy widely entertained during the seventeenth century), replies that in several respects the Greeks and Romans came short of the perfection demanded by the rules. Their playwrights did not adhere invariably to the unity of time; unity of place is a modern beauty not even mentioned by their critics; their plots are sometimes so ineptly adapted to the time and place restrictions as to force them into gross impossibilities. Besides these faults of contrivance, their exclusive reenactment of known fables, or, in comedy, of a few conventional plot situations robbed their plays of all suspense, so that the audience "sat with a yawning kind of expectation." Most damning of all, "they have often shown a prosperous wickedness, and an unhappy piety," thus subverting the poet's cardinal duty of moral instruction.

The Crites-Eugenius exchange has an obvious place in the century-long quarrel between the Ancients and the Moderns that vexed literary discussion in France especially and was belatedly satirized in Swift's *Battle of the Books* (1704). Issues of more enduring import underlie the debate between the two other speakers. Lisideius praises the French dramatists for surpassing the ancients in their rigorous observance of the unities of time and place. In the crucial element of action their productions are models of regularity. Unity of action in a French play is never weakened by a double plot, nor is its effect diluted by the "unnatural mixture" of comedy and tragedy. Decorum is never sacrificed to that other English theatrical vice, on-stage violence. In short, Lisideius makes the case for the austere formalism that had recently been extolled by the Abbé d'Aubignac in his *Pratique du théâtre,* and of which, as René Bray suggests,[1] Racine's *Bérénice* (1670) is perhaps the ultimate realization.

There is, however, another ideal. Or perhaps it is the same ideal, dramatic mimesis, the *"just* and *lively* image of human nature,"* differently conceived, the issue being only which adjective to stress. Lisideius had clearly preferred *just.* Neander, though he acknowledges the virtues of French regularity and decorum, signals the alternate emphasis at the very beginning of his discourse:

> For the lively imitation of nature being in the definition of a play, those which best fulfill that law ought to be esteemed superior to the others. 'T is true, those beauties of the French poesy are such as will raise perfection

> higher where it is, but are not sufficient to give it where
> it is not: they are indeed the beauties of a statue, but
> not of a man. . . .

The "beauties of a statue, but not of a man." Metaphorical
correlatives of *just* and *lively*, Neander's expressions sym-
bolize the dialectic quality of the neoclassical aesthetic,
which sought constantly to reconcile the formal and the
natural. Here he leans toward the lifelike in order to
assert the superiority of English dramatic freedom over
French restraint, of tragi-comedy over purity of genre, of
variety over concentration.

At the same time it is important to notice that none of
Dryden's arguments rests exclusively on the criterion of
what is closest to real life. Dr. Johnson was later to defend tragi-comedy on the ground that mirth and sorrow
exist together in real experience. Not so Dryden. His appeal is to the capacities of the imagination. Lisideius had
voiced the familiar charge that comic and serious elements in a single play cancel each other's effect. But,
asks Neander, "why should he imagine the soul of man
more heavy than his senses? Does not the eye pass from
an unpleasant object to a pleasant in a much shorter time
than is required to this?" To this psychological argument
he adds an aesthetic one: "does not the unpleasantness of
the first commend the beauty of the latter?" since "con-
traries, when placed near, set off each other." Similarly,
his defense of English double plots rests not on their
superior verisimilitude but on their partaking of a more
complex order, an order whose type exists in nature itself. In the contrary motions of the planets he finds an
analogy to the separate movements of the main and sub-
ordinate plots of an English play.

Neander objects to the French playwrights' "servile
observations" of the unities of time and place. Here
Dryden is able to quote Corneille himself in support of
his contention that in their zeal for strict adherence to
these unities the French have sacrificed too many beauties and committed too many absurdities. Yet if Dryden

had not shared the general faith of his age in the efficacy of these rules themselves he would not have included in the *Essay* Neander's detailed *examen* of Ben Jonson's *Epicoene, or, The Silent Woman,* in which he takes some patriotic pride in showing how skillfully an English poet *could* follow them when he chose to do so. If in this same *Essay* he can without inconsistency also utter his famous eulogy of "the incomparable Shakespeare," whose defiance of the unities so scandalized Restoration taste, it is owing to his sound judgment that however useful these mechanical rules might be, they were not essential.

But apart from his moderate position on the rules, and apart from his ready appreciation of the Elizabethan achievement, there is something else. Dryden knew that when the claims of form and order are granted, there is always the danger of arid formalism. He protests against the long-winded set speeches of French tragedy because "it is unnatural for anyone in a gust of passion to speak long together." Though this objection now seems hardly relevant to the peculiar art of the French classical theater, the point was shrewdly taken. And in any case Dryden immediately concedes the relativity of his verdict by noting how much it owes to national differences. The "gay and airy" French temperament, he observes, requires the corrective of such grave hundred-line tirades, whereas the "more sullen" English go to the theater for diversion.

As much interest as these problems retain for the modern reader, they account far less for the enduring value of Dryden's critical thought than the final controversy between Crites and Neander over the use of rhyme in serious plays. The question engages his attention in the earlier Preface to *The Rival Ladies* (1668) and in the *Defence of an Essay* later in that same year. To gauge its full significance requires a look not merely at this latter critical piece but at an important aspect of Dryden's dramatic practice as well.

Crites makes the plausible point that blank verse ought to be employed in tragedies as it is in comedies, being closer than rhyming couplets are to living speech. Since a play is an imitation of real life it ought to be as lifelike as possible. Rhyme, so manifestly the result of prior agreement among the actors, nullifies the illusion of unpremeditated dialogue. When one considers Dryden's mastery of the technique, it is probably true that he had, as T. S. Eliot suggested, a personal interest in urging its general adoption on the stage. But the arguments he advances stand in their own right as valid critical principles independently of any personal motivation. With obvious relish of his deductive skill, Neander retorts that if no man ever speaks in rhyme, neither does he speak in blank verse. If a tragedy is "the representation of Nature, 'tis Nature wrought up to an higher pitch. The Plot, the characters, the wit, the passions, the descriptions, are all exalted above the level of common converse, as high as the imagination of the poet can carry them, with proportion to verisimilitude." Rhyme is therefore natural, he concludes, to the high dignity of the tragic genre.

Though the critical vocabulary of his day is inadequate to the conception, it is clear enough that Dryden has grasped the crucial distinction between art and life. If no one during his time took "imitation of nature" to mean a literal replica of reality, the impossible goal of nineteenth-century realists, no other neoclassical critic so cogently exposed its fallacy. Almost a century before the invention of the word, Dryden had a fundamentally sound insight into the conditions of the aesthetic, into certain requirements of form that literature shares with other mimetic arts. Thus his analogies to sculpture and the dance: to imitate nature properly a play must be "set above it; as statues which are placed on high are made greater than the life, that they may descend to the sight in their just proportion." To Crites' objection that rhymed conversation on the stage, being obviously contrived, destroys the illusion of spontaneity, Dryden's reply is incontrovertible by the measure of all we have since discovered about the value of the formal distortion that life necessarily undergoes in artistic representation. Why, Neander demands, should this contrived effect

> be more displeasing to you than in a dance which is well contrived? You see there the united design of many persons to make up one figure . . . the confederacy is plain amongst them, for chance could never produce any thing so beautiful. . . .

The original of Crites, Dryden's brother-in-law Sir Robert Howard, whose protests against rhyming drama had been aired earlier in his *Preface to Four New Plays* (1665), answered Dryden's arguments in the Preface to his play *The Great Favorite* (1668). When a second edition of Dryden's *The Indian Emperor* appeared in the same year, he seized the opportunity to have the last word by introducing it with *A Defence of An Essay of Dramatic Poesy*. Though marred by a sarcasm generated in the heat of what had become a personal quarrel, the *Defence* adds significantly to Dryden's mimetic theory. He concedes that the poet must imitate well:

> but to affect the soul, and excite the passions, and, above all, to move admiration . . . a bare imitation will not serve.

And he goes further, to affirm that prose is improper in a serious play for the very reason that it is too close to conversation: "there may be too great a likeness," he dares to say, in poetry as in portrait painting. Even in comedy, where prose is admitted, some distance between art and life must be kept. In his *Bartholomew Fair* Ben Jonson could never have delighted his audience "had he only said or done those very things that are daily spoken or practiced in the fair"; otherwise the real fair would be as pleasing as the play, which it is manifestly not. Dryden has only to follow the lead of his own impeccable logic in order to discredit once and for all the inadequacy of Howard's naive conception of artistic imitation. Like so many others before and since, Sir Robert forgets that through the agency of the creative imagination the dull and tawdry in life is transmuted into something rich and precious. Dryden knows this fact to be crucial for any valid aesthetic. Jonson's comedy is an example; "the copy," he remarks, "is of price, though the original be vile."

Yet a problem remains. How are we to reconcile a favorable estimate of the theoretical grounds of Dryden's defense of rhymed drama with the relative failure of his own rhyming heroic plays? Not only do the chiming couplets of *The Conquest of Granada,* for example, strike us as stilted and even ludicrous, but we know that Dryden achieved his one undoubted success in tragedy only with *All for Love* (1678), in which he abandoned rhyme for blank verse, in conscious emulation of Shakespeare. Moreover, the finest tragedies not only of the pre-Restoration English theater but of Dryden's own period, those by his rival Thomas Otway and his successor Nicholas Rowe, are in blank verse. By Dr. Johnson's day the general view was that rhyme was simply out of place on the stage (one of Dick Minim's critical commonplaces).

In the first place, students of the English heroic play tell us, Dryden's rhymed tragedies were quite popular with audiences while the vogue lasted. He turned to blank verse, they explain, only when heroic tragedy was supplanted by a tragedy of sentiment designed to elicit sympathy rather than admiration. This new type involved a degree of naturalism to which, Dryden recognized, rhyme was inappropriate.[2] Though this account is entirely borne out by the facts, it doesn't take us very far. We still have to explain why the heroic drama itself is of such poor quality, because whatever its momentary popularity when new, there is no use pretending that anyone finds much genuine pleasure in it today. Something may still be said for the prosodic relativism of those who, like Richard Hurd, suggested that rhyme pleases in French because it supplies a deficiency in that language, whereas in richer English it can only be an "idle affection." Yet it seems odd that anyone as sensitive as Dryden was to the peculiar qualities of various languages would not have grasped this fact. Besides, if Hurd's explanation is sufficient, would it not similarly invalidate rhyme in English nondramatic verse, where however it continues to be highly effective down to the present moment?

Actually, the failure in application of a fundamentally sound theory can best be explained not by a bald comparison of doctrine and practice, but by examining Dryden's heroic plays themselves. The principle that Dryden rightly glimpsed when he insisted that dramatic dialogue be elevated above ordinary conversation is an instance of what has since been called aesthetic distance. His error lay in failing to see that the device of rhyme conferred *a degree of distance disproportionate to the other elements in his plays.** His Almanzors and Benzaydas, for all their lofty concernments, are in outward deportment actually at a lesser remove from the familiar than is compatible with the highly stylized mode of expression imposed on them by rhyme. The result is a tonal inconsistency, not infrequent in literary history, that invited the barbs of *The Rehearsal*. The valid objection, then as now, is not that kings and princesses in the real world never spoke like this, but that these particular kings and princesses of Dryden's imagined world *would* not have done so. On the stages of Corneille and Racine, with their more decorous, less bustling, altogether more rarefied mimesis of reality, rhyme was almost as necessary as it was unsuited to the livelier, more naturalized English stage tradition to which Dryden was a willing heir.

The Prologue to *Secret Love* (1668) suggests that he

___

* A similar error, among others perhaps, seems to account for the unfortunate rhetorical impression given by Maxwell Anderson's attempt to adapt pseudo-Shakespearian blank verse to naturalistic characters and themes of social protest.

thought the special excellences of the French and English stages could be successfully united, since he consciously sought

> a mingled chime
> Of Jonson's humour with Corneille's rhyme.

And in *Of Heroic Plays* (1672), after crediting Davenant, the inventor of the form, with having heightened his characters "from the example of Corneille and some French poets," he excuses his own fondness for drums, trumpets, and battle scenes by the precedent of Shakespeare and Jonson. It was an experiment doomed to failure from the start. Rodrigue and Chimène, the protagonists of Corneille's *Le Cid,* are genuinely heroic. They are not real people placed in the common field of life; they are ideal figures dwelling in the imaginary garden of the poet's feigning. They are *literally* and purely bound by a code of chivalric behavior that in real life was never more than an abstract ideal even among the medieval Spanish aristocracy. Overt action, such as Rodrigue's fatal duel with his prospective father-in-law, is kept off stage not only in conformity with French stage decorum but because the dramatic interest, as Daniel Mornet pointed out, attaches not to the physical event but to the mental anguish of soul-rending moral decisions which constitute the real toad in Corneille's imaginary garden. All else, the decora of social relations, of speech, of gesture, is on a plane of artificiality and stylization raised as far above reality as neoclassical *vraisemblance* would allow; and this is the plane proper to rhyme.

The conditions of Dryden's heroic drama are almost exactly the reverse. What reality there is in *The Conquest of Granada,* though it is hardly convincing, lies in the outward events, in action and utterance, while what is most artificial, and artificial in the worst sense, is the interior movement of feeling and morality. In this way Dryden's heroic tragedy comes very close to offering us a would-be live garden inhabited by an imaginary toad.

In *The Conquest of Granada,* this unfortunate situation is aggravated by the hero. Almanzor cannot be truly heroic because he is not tragic. His boundless defiance of every law but his own will is a real-life trait exaggerated to caricature. In other words it is a "humour," like those of Ben Jonson's comic characters. Northrop Frye notes in Marlowe's Tamberlaine and Shakespeare's Othello "the touch of *miles gloriosus,*" [3] the comic type of the boasting soldier derived from Plautine comedy. Almanzor is saved from being a *miles gloriosus* pure and simple because his deeds are as good as his words—and as extravagant. Even so, he is in effect more nearly a comic than a tragic character, and therefore closer in what he says and does to ordinary life than any tragic character can afford to be. So close in fact that his rhymed speech gives the impression of somebody "talking poetry," which is an affectation and therefore ludicrous.

Aureng-Zebe (1675) represents Dryden's final attempt to adapt the convention of rhyme to the English stage. Though superior to his earlier attempts, it too, as Dryden realized at the time, was unsatisfactory. Only with the blank verse of *All for Love* did he attain, in Moody E. Prior's words, "the ease of unstudied discourse with all the studied complexity of poetry . . . the ultimate relationship between the possibilities of the language and the demands of the form. . . ." [4]

Dryden's superiority to other critics of his generation is as apparent in his practical criticism as in his theory. Though there are the lapses and contradictions to be expected in a record of thirty-five years, most of his specific judgments and analyses of poets past and contemporary require small correction and no apology. In many of them the taste of his age is tempered by his own appreciative skill. In some, as in the celebrated encomium of Shakespeare in *An Essay of Dramatic Poesy,* it is clearly transcended. That single paragraph of tribute so far set the theme of the neoclassical estimate of his country's greatest poet that the most characteristic Shakespeare criticism for a century following reads in praise and blame like a commentary on Dryden's text. His glowing words are among the most familiar in the history of criticism. Shakespeare is "the man who of all modern, and perhaps ancient poets, had the largest and most comprehensive soul. . . . when he describes anything, you more than see it, you feel it too." The remarkable thing is that he wrote and published them not only decades before there was any cult of The Bard but when in fact dramatic theory and cultivated taste were alike inimical to the art of Shakespeare and his fellows. Dryden himself understandably felt the force of this bias, which can show itself as much in his remarks on Shakespeare as anywhere else. Surveying Elizabethan drama in 1672, he condemns the plots of *A Winter's Tale* and *Measure for Measure* as "grounded on impossibilities" or else "meanly written." The history plays, he feels called upon to notice, violate the unity of time. At no time of his career, however, did such attitudes prevent him from according Shakespeare the very highest rank. Writing to John Dennis after reading the wholesale attack on *Othello* in Rymer's *Short View of Tragedy,* he declares that Shakespeare had a true genius for tragedy. Though many of the faults noted by Rymer "are truly there, . . . who will read Mr. Rymer or not read Shakespeare?"

Though he admired Spenser's versification, in his general estimate of *The Faerie Queene* Dryden is otherwise the prisoner of the idea of epic unity entertained in his day. Spenser's poem has too many heroes. Most of what Dryden says of Milton's *Paradise Lost* is governed by the same preconception. In addition, he deplores the poem's lack of a heroic subject and its oversupply of machines (supernatural agents). The language of *Paradise Lost* struck him as antiquated and harsh-sounding and he disapproved of Milton's use of blank verse. Yet none of these reservations made late in life suggests any retraction of the opinion he had expressed in the Preface to *The State of Innocence* (1677), his operatic version of *Paradise Lost,* that it was "undoubtedly one of the greatest, most noble, and most sublime" of English poems.

Deservedly better known is the critique of Chaucer's *The Canterbury Tales* mentioned above. This critical gem is a model of a distinctive type of practical criticism that may loosely be styled criticism by description. It consists not so much in analysis as in giving a character (in the seventeenth-century sense) of the work under scrutiny. The effect is to throw into telling relief whatever is unique in a given piece or writer. In a critic like William Hazlitt, endowed with an unusually sympathetic imagination, the procedure may amount to a succinct prose equivalent of a poem. It is a kind of enlightened impressionism that sends the reader back to the work with a heightened awareness of its peculiar appeal. In the literary portraits of Sainte-Beuve the method received its subtlest elaboration. Edmund Wilson is among its ablest modern exponents.

The best way of showing any critic's practical skill is of course to let him speak for himself. Dryden on Chaucer's pilgrims is too well known as an anthology staple to warrant extensive quotation. A passage on Samuel Butler's *Hudibras,* though less memorable, may equally illustrate the critic's gift for evaluative description. It occurs in the *Discourse Concerning Satire:*

> The choice of his numbers is suitable enough to his design, as he has managed it; but in any other hand, the shortness of his verse, and the quick returns of rhyme, had debased the dignity of style. And besides, the double rhyme (a necessary companion of burlesque writing) is not so proper for manly satire; for it turns earnest too much to jest, and gives us a boyish kind of pleasure. It tickles awkwardly with a kind of pain, to the best sort of readers: we are pleased ungratefully and, if I may say so, against our liking. . . . 'Tis, indeed, below so great a master to make use of such a little instrument. But his good sense is perpetually shining through all he writes; it affords us not the time of finding faults. We pass through the levity of his rhyme,

and are immediately carried into some admirable, useful
thought.

The fresher one is from reading *Hudibras* itself, the more
accurate will this characterization appear to be. Readers
whose Latin permits them to do so may put many of
Dryden's pronouncements on Virgil, of whom he professed himself "a religious admirer," to the same test of
immediate appeal to the passage in question.

Certain obvious inconsistencies and shifts of position
in Dryden's critical writings have been charged too heavily
against him. The usual indictment overlooks the fact
that his career opened on the eve of a literary evolution
only less profound than the revolutions later presided
over by Wordsworth and T. S. Eliot. Dryden's burden
was to establish a new poetic idiom to replace the old
one that had finally exhausted itself in Abraham Cowley,
in order, as he somewhat narrowly expressed it, "To
please an age more gallant than the last." In such circumstances, false starts, shifts of emphasis or opinion, and
hesitancy to challenge authoritative pronouncement are
inevitable. There is, for example, a marked discrepancy
between the mild dissent from Rymer's *Tragedies of the
Last Age* registered in *The Grounds of Criticism in
Tragedy* and the bold refutation known as *The Heads
of an Answer to Rymer* which he chose never to publish.
Yet the easy hindsight by which we prefer the *Heads*
to the published *Grounds* does not justify castigating as
lack of candor in Dryden what may well have been the
honest diffidence of a skeptical mind. Granted, it is disappointing to find him during his last decade damning
tragi-comedy as "wholly Gothic," and by the tiresome old
argument that "mirth and gravity destroy each other."
But such chilling betrayals of his own best insights are
remarkably rare.

The typical Dryden is the better Dryden, whose critical
penetration is never more evident than in the frequency
with which he perceived and defined the limitations of
the very aesthetic of which he remains the first great

spokesman. It is the Dryden who in that heyday of literary didacticism sensed the danger of debasing poetry to propaganda. He laments that the Roman poet Lucretius, whom he admired and translated, "aimed more to instruct in his System of Nature than to delight," and "was so much an atheist that he forgot sometimes to be a poet." This adulteration of art by polemic intent was to be Matthew Arnold's charge against Wordsworth's *Excursion,* but from the author of *Religio Laici* and *The Hind and the Panther,* who was never so much the orthodox Christian that *he* forgot to be a poet, it comes with the better grace.

IV *THE RATIONALE OF IMITATION*

THE MATRIX OF THEORY

Like the aesthetic of rules, the neoclassic faith in the imitation of literary models was a legacy of Renaissance Italy passed on by the Elizabethans. Sir Philip Sidney had given imitation an equal place with "art" and exercise in the discipline of the poet; and Ben Jonson had included it among the five requisites for poetic success, defining it as a poet's ability to convert the substance of another poet to his own use. By Restoration times the doctrine had long been familiar to Western Europe, frequently advocated, occasionally challenged, and both honored and dishonored in practice. Today of course the idea that an aspiring writer should deliberately set out to produce something that bore a noticeable resemblance to the work of one of his predecessors strikes most people as a grotesque prostitution of personal talent. Later on in this chapter I shall offer reasons for qualifying this hostile reaction or abandoning it once and for all to its nineteenth-century progenitors. In the meanwhile, however, it does seem fair to ask why the subjects of Charles II, who as Dryden observed lived in an age so skeptical that they took nothing from the past on faith, weren't as impatient to jettison this idea as they were to pass beyond the science, philosophy, and literary taste of their ancestors. Or, since a few of them *were* so inclined, the question becomes why they failed to carry the day.

The explanation is really plain enough. As with the rules, several aspects of the contemporary intellectual climate tended to accredit the venerable doctrine. The models proposed for imitation were primarily certain ancient Greek and Roman masterpieces. And the first thing to recall—and the easiest for today's classically illiterate student to overlook—is that during this period many educated people read those classics in the original languages with mingled delight and envy. No doubt to a small class of men a thorough knowledge of classical literature was simply a matter of bread and butter, as to another a superficial familiarity with it was a requisite of social polish. No doubt too, many people simply lauded what they heard others laud. But when we read in Tobias Smollett's *Peregrine Pickle* of the young man who deemed it "his duty to magnify the ancients above all competition, with an affected fervor," we recognize his affectation as the predictable spawn of repeated expressions of genuine admiration. So strong was this admiration that to suppose a work like the *Iliad* or the *Georgics* might double for nature itself as inspiration and model for the poet seemed a good deal less preposterous than it does now. Pope's equation of Nature and Homer, in *An Essay on Criticism*, gains force by being read in the context of the passage that begins with line 181:

> Still green with bays each ancient Altar stands.

Even if the obeisance here paid to the great pagan masters was a tradition the youthful author of an *ars poetica* would hardly dare flout by omitting it, no reader of these fervid lines can mistake the ardent sincerity of Pope's tribute. Joseph Spence speaks in the *Anecdotes* of his once bursting into tears while reading the passage in the *Iliad* on Priam's grief over the death of his son Hector. This sensitivity to the abiding power of classical literary art was by no means peculiar to Pope, although, significantly, it seems to have been clearest in those who, like him, "knew themselves to sing." When, at the height of his own poetic mastery, Dryden set out to translate the *Aeneid,* he wondered aloud (as it were) how he could rise to the sublimity of Virgil's thought and diction. Quoting one verse "amongst a thousand others," he asks what modern poet or language can capture in translation its majestic beauty. "For my part," he confesses in one of those touches that endear Dryden to a reader, "I am lost in the admiration of it. I contemn the world when I think on it, and myself when I translate it." If the by then celebrated Dryden (it was the year of *Alexander's Feast,* 1697) could write thus, a modern reader may be more inclined to forgive the young and unknown author of *Annus Mirabilis* (1667) for being eager to direct public attention to the fact that many of the images in that poem were copied from Virgil "and the rest . . . imitations of him."

Naturally, adulation of the classics was by no means universal on either side of the English Channel. Some of the so-called Moderns, like Charles Perrault in France, spoke out for the equality or superiority of modern learning and letters over the ancient. Others, not readily rangeable on either side in the battle of the books, agreed that this might in fact be true for certain genres, drama for example, though not for all or most of them. What is especially notable is that very few even of those who considered themselves in most respects Moderns denied the generally preeminent quality of Greek and Roman writing. William Wotton, no adherent of the Ancient party, argued in his *Reflections on Ancient and Modern Learning* (1694) that a deep regard for the classics was no blind prejudice, and that the best modern authors have been those most careful to imitate them. Most telling of all, Wotton points out that Perrault and his fellow detractors of the ancients in France had read the Greek and Latin works only in French translations, some of them prose versions of poetic originals! In similar vein, Dryden was later to observe that Englishmen who knew Homer and Virgil only in John Ogilby's wretched English versions could hardly be expected to understand why poets like himself prized those masters so highly.

In any case, the argument for imitating the ancients rested on more than the common experience of what Robert Wolseley called their "unaccountable Magick." The alternative demand for originality was thought to be a demand for what was impossible, or only minimally possible. Addison, who reviewed Pope's *An Essay on Criticism* in *Spectator* 253, praised it especially for expressing familiar ideas in a new and graceful manner. This thought led him to remind his readers that it had become impossible for mankind to discover anything new in criticism, or for that matter in morals, art, or science. "We have little left us, but to represent the common Sense of Mankind in more strong, more beautiful, or more uncommon Lights." To have represented traditional human passion and thought in an unusually attractive form is at least an apt description of the literary achievement of Addison's own century. Slightly altering Pope's better known phrasing of the idea, the "true wit" of *Gulliver's Travels,* of Pope's own *Dunciad* and moral poems, and of Dr. Johnson's poems and essays, is surely "what oft was thought but *seldom* so well expressed." But though the belief that *tout est dit* may have had a certain salutary effect on neoclassical literature by endowing it with a peculiar quality it might otherwise have missed, it is certain that it tended to disparage originality or at best severely restrict its permissible range. As usual, a certain broad logic underlay this attitude. The argument ran that since modern psychology had shown human reason to be always and everywhere the same, and truth thus one and universal, anything that was entirely new or original could hardly avoid being false or eccentric. Even the defenders of originality and "invention" seldom envisaged a novelty radically nonconformist; most of them called only for some kind of revitalizing of traditional forms and formulas. Variously described by English eighteenth-century critics, this inventive imitation was most memorably expressed in a line of André Chénier's poem *l'Invention*:

> Sur des pensers nouveaux faisons des vers antiques.*

How far Chénier's originality was circumscribed by tradition can be seen from the immediately preceding line, which urges the modern poet to kindle his torch at ancient poetic fires. There is a certain ironic appropriateness in Chénier's dying at last on the guillotine, victim of an extension into politics of the radical "originality" he opposed.

The growing dissatisfaction with literary imitation during the latter half of the century by no means put an end to the views espoused by the generation of Addison and Pope. Dr. Johnson, though he scorned imitators and placed a special premium on novelty, admitted in *Rambler* 143 that even in the most original of books "there is little new beyond the disposition of materials already provided. . . ." Richard Hurd thought the same. In *Discourse on Poetical Imitation* (1751) he went so far as to declare that even Homer and Shakespeare owed their superiority not to having discovered new thoughts and images but to their striking way of conveying old ones. In such circumstances no other road to success was open to a young poet than to form himself on whatever model seemed most congenial to his own aims and powers.

Unless, that is, he happened to be that rare thing called a genius. Though the genius was not always defined in quite the same way in neoclassical discussion, one of the attributes usually ascribed to him was a superior power of inventiveness that allowed him both to disregard the rules of art and to defy imitation. He was, in short, an Original. Homer, Shakespeare, and the authors of the Old Testament were the few examples repeatedly cited. Some scholars have pointed to the enthusiastic

* From new ideas let us make ancient verses.

praise accorded these creative giants in order either to convict the best neoclassical critics of self-contradiction or to range them quite simply on the side of originality and against imitation. Although neither of these conclusions is accurate, it is easy to see how they arose. Exalting Homer for his fertile invention, Pope showed in the Preface to his *Iliad* how Virgil and other epic poets only imitated his design and episodes. Addison identified two classes of genius: to the first belong Homer, Pindar, and Shakespeare, all "originals"; to the second belong those who follow the rules, the "imitators." Anyone may be excused for inferring from *Spectator* 160, where these opinions occur, that Addison clearly regarded imitative authors as an inferior kind. An imitation, he expressly declares, is "not to compare with a good Original," adding that every writer of merit always has something of his own. Yet when he comes to his second class of genius, he is careful to say that they are not "inferior to the first," but only "of a different kind." In the light of this qualification it seems proper to conclude that an imitative work is not to compare with an original because the two are incommensurable, not because one is superior to the other. Addison's inclusion of Plato, Aristotle, Virgil, Cicero, and Milton (hardly second-raters by anybody's measure) among the imitators strongly suggests that this was his meaning. Pope's comparison of Homer and Virgil is similar. He does not, he says, mean to disparage Virgil for having followed his great model. If the Roman poet lacks a quality admirable in the Greek, he has compensating virtues of his own: "Homer was the greater genius, Virgil the better artist."

The discrimination of qualities that Pope and Addison were at pains to clarify actually betrays an irreducible ambivalence of aesthetic standards that runs throughout neoclassicism and beyond. It is foreshadowed in Dryden's contrast of Shakespeare and Jonson: the innocently original, irregular, and therefore faulty genius over against the deliberately imitative, regular and therefore "correct"

artist. Dryden saw Shakespeare and Jonson as respectively
the Homer and Virgil of his country's literature, and if
he freely confesses his love for the former he was nonetheless unable to conceal his admiration for Ben. This
Homer-Virgil contrast (in which a predilection for either
one seems to depend on the reigning taste or else on
nothing more than private temperament or momentary
mood) was not confined to literature or to England. Sir
Joshua Reynolds differentiated Michelangelo, the Homer
of painting, from the "Virgilian" Raphael. Raphael's
having formed himself on Masaccio and others did not
prevent Sir Joshua at one stage of his career from naming
him the greatest of painters, although he was later to exalt
his "truly divine" rival. In France, partisans of the "bold"
Corneille advanced his claims against those who considered the elegantly correct Racine's plays to be the
epitome of the tragic art. In the nineteenth century
Sainte-Beuve found it still valid to distinguish two "glori-
ous families" in Western literary history, one of which is
headed by Homer, with Aeschylus, Dante, Shakespeare,
and Corneille among his descendants. Virgil, whom
Sainte-Beuve styles at once imitative and inventive, is the
grand progenitor of the other, fathering Tasso, Boileau,
and above all Racine.

In Restoration and Augustan England, protests against
imitation, like those against the rules, were called forth
mainly by abuses of it, by tasteless aping of the outward
effects or incidental techniques of the chosen model.
Admittedly the principle was two-sided, a blessing to
the gifted, a bane to the man of slender talents. To imitation, René Bray was convinced, France owes the masterpieces of her classical literature. Yet he also shows how
in the face of constant critical warnings against mistaking
servile copying for "l'imitation libérale" there appeared a
host of modern epics, like Chapelain's *La Pucelle*, that
were hardly more than lifeless travesties of the *Aeneid;*
and many a would-be tragedian followed Roman Sen-
eca into deserved obscurity.[1] Though there was less

of this in England, it did exist. In *Rambler* 158 Dr. Johnson expressed his disgust with epic poets whose reverence for ancient example went to the superstitious length of imitating the very number of books comprising the original. He may have been thinking of Cowley, who planned his *Davideis* in twelve books, "after the *Patern* of our Master *Virgil*. . . ." In less blatant cases it is not always easy to decide whether one has to do with sincere and fecundating emulation or with self-debasing obsequiousness, as when Thomas Shadwell worries about being thought impudent for daring to imitate the matchless Ben Jonson in his comedies.

Although some writers challenged the imitation of models only because of the sins committed in its name, a few did defy the principle itself. These latter elicited counterarguments, like those advanced by Reynolds in the *Discourses,* which possess enduring theoretical interest. Appeals to self-reliance and condemnations of "a slavish bigotry to the ancients," such as those in a plea for the "liberty" of writing made by Samuel Cobb in 1701, have a specious plausibility about them that frequently disappears on closer inspection. In like manner it may seem at first impossible to withhold approval from the brave call for literary independence that William Davenant put forth in the Preface to his *Gondibert,* in which he damned imitation as a bar to progress and discovery. Nevertheless—charitably waiving the question as to the value of whatever is "discovered" in *Gondibert* itself—we may wish to weigh his statement that no writer can excel those he imitates. Reynolds, over a century later, sought to indoctrinate the art students at the Royal Academy with the opposite notion that progress can be made *only* by imitating, since without it an art must remain forever in its infancy. Or, if artistic progress is an idea too vague and suspect, we may take Davenant's "excell" to mean "do the same thing better"; to be guided by existing example, in other words, is to relinquish all hope of superior achievement. Yet it does not seem extravagant to value Pope's *Essay on Criticism* above the several verse "poetic arts" it quite consciously imitates, or to say that *The Rape of the Lock* is an advance over those earlier mock epics, Boileau's *Le Lutrin* and Samuel Garth's *The Dispensary,* without which it could perhaps not have come into being, into such "being" as it actually attained.

What then of Edward Young's celebrated *Conjectures on Original Composition* (1759), long hailed as an attack on the principle of literary imitation? Though some of Young's friends must have demurred at his reservations about Pope, on the theoretical level there is little in this essay that had not been an accepted commonplace for many years. It extols originality, as almost everyone else had been doing; it sets original pieces above the imitative kind, a preference often expressed before; and although, again like many other writers, Young condemns slavish and mechanical copying, he by no means opposes imitation itself. On the contrary, he endorses the chief articles of its creed. Far from scorning the Ancients, he insists that whoever doesn't admire them confesses his own ignorance. If it is the lot of most writers to be imitators, it is often an honorable lot, some imitators, like Pope, being "most excellent, and even immortal." Adopting a well-known concept from Longinus' *On the Sublime,* Young urges writers to compose "with the spirit and taste of the ancients," though not with their materials; to imitate Homer, not the *Iliad.* His one contribution, which was to bear fruit in the next age (especially in Germany), was his glimpse of organicism: he sees that a true literary work is not a mechanical composite, but "of a vegetable nature . . . it grows, it is not made."

Despite this insight, however, Young was no Romantic born ahead of his time. The *Conjectures* is part of the flood of eighteenth-century books and essays on original genius. He is also very much of his own time in being obviously motivated in part by the growing post-Augustan taste for the natural, the pathetic, and the sentimental.

Addison's *Cato,* he complains, though otherwise admirable, leaves the audience dry-eyed. He even repeats the contemporary misjudgment that Shakespeare is entirely original whereas Jonson is "as much an imitator."

TRADITION AND GENRE

On balance, it can be said that the imitation doctrine did more good than harm to the creative writers who subscribed to it. Its effect on literary criticism was at least equally beneficial. In perfect keeping with the cosmology of the day, the very idea of imitating models implies and depends on a conception of literature as constituting a total order, a system of genres, in which each work, however unique, is related by a kind of family resemblance to all the other works in its genre and ultimately to the whole of literature. It is worth noting among other practical benefits that this conception encouraged the early appearance of comparative criticism. Only on the assumption of an orderly literary totality could Dryden have offered his comparison of Chaucer and Ovid, or Dr. Johnson his of Dryden and Pope, as meaningful. The imitation doctrine sanctioned Rymer's skillful evaluative comparison, in the Preface to his translation of Rapin's *Reflections on Aristotle's Poetics* (1674), of the epic descriptions of night by Virgil, Tasso, Marino, Chapelain, Le Moyne, and Dryden. The later examples which he quotes may be regarded as "imitations" of one or more of the earlier ones, and whether they go beyond or fall short of their predecessors—Rymer's immediate concern—they are subject to comparative scrutiny because they all affect a traditional manner of treating an identical subject in epic verse. Since the dissolution of the harmonious universe of the Enlightenment, of which the literary order was a type, comparative criticism has necessarily become correspondingly more self-conscious and subjective.

Another premise of the doctrine of imitation was recognized by certain critics at the time to be subject to some qualification. Against the belief in a universal norm of wit and good sense, there was the growing perception that the forms of literature, including the genres themselves, were conditioned by the temporal and local environments in which they were produced. Seventeenth-century French critics had recognized that changes in taste imposed a limit on following the ancients. St. Evremond pointed out that Sophocles' *Oedipus Rex,* which was the model of tragic perfection for Aristotle, would disgust and horrify a modern audience in French translation. Critics who investigated the relationship between books and institutions, later and ever since called historical critics, were therefore not long in challenging the exponents of imitation both to moderate their claims and to attempt a more sophisticated justification of their faith in the process. (This latter undertaking neoclassicism never quite achieved.) Thomas Blackwell, whose *Inquiry into the Life and Writings of Homer* (1735) was one of the best and earliest examples of this kind of criticism, decided that the epic poem was now extinct because the peace and security of modern society had abolished the marvelous and surprising events on which that genre had subsisted. Blackwell cites the example of Giovanni Trissino, who in disregard of historical change tried to imitate Homer, as nearly as possible reproducing the material and manner of his great model, only replacing his pagan gods and furies with Christian angels and devils. The result, Blackwell thought, was that the native Italian spirit and force that captivates readers of Dante and Ariosto was in Trissino's case "crushed by imitation." Not so, he adds, with *The Way of the World* and *The Rape of the Lock,* works that drew their content and spirit from the authors' direct observation of society.

Despite the considerable force of this deepening historical sense, the conviction prevailed that with due allowance made for variety in manners and creeds human nature was what it had been always and everywhere.

This constancy was the guarantee of that stream of tradition, choked and muddied only by the Gothic enthusiasm of the Middle Ages, which neoclassical literary men saw flowing from the wellspring of Homer down through the best work of their own time. A modern student will be quick to object to this vision as fostering a much oversimplified conception of how literary past and present are related. But he ought at the same time to see how in the minds of men who entertained it the poet could have no loftier aim than to keep this proud tradition alive by extending it. Imitation, the method for accomplishing this aim, prescribed that a writer steep himself in those masterpieces which best embodied the tradition, as a preparation for giving it fresh embodiment in the idiom of his own time and people. Looked at from the viewpoint of the poet's psychology, it is obvious that the attitude appropriate to this aspiration would be not servility but a combination of humility and confidence. The humility would come from the aspirant's realization that the established models were indeed worthy of the emulation which a confidence in his own gifts spurred him to undertake.

In this regard classical self-confidence should be carefully distinguished from pseudoromantic artistic egotism. In *Paradise Lost* Milton declared his purpose to be nothing less than to achieve "Things unattempted yet in prose or rhyme," and it is hard to think of any equal in English literature to John Milton's towering self-assurance. While thinking of himself as the successor and challenger of Homer and Virgil, however, he was also glad to hail them as the nourishers of his own powers. According to the pseudoromantic conception, on the other hand, the poet pretends to a unique creation drawn exclusively from the private resources of his own soul, apparently oblivious of how much that soul was constituted of what he had read by others. I use the awkward term "pseudoromantic" because the greatest romantic writers themselves held no such solipsistic view of the matter as I have described. At their maturest and best they were at least aware of seeking membership in a proud and exclusive company. One recalls the young Keats' poignant words in a letter to his brother George: "I think I shall be among the English Poets after my death."

On the whole, neoclassical explanations and defenses of literary imitation imperfectly represent the degree of creative skill demanded by the process. To see this clearly we need to examine what a highly gifted poet actually produced as a result of it. Pope's several imitations of Horace do not give the impression of being derivative work; on the contrary they seem everywhere marked by a force and style peculiarly his own. Moreover, even if we compare the imitation with the model, for example the *Epistle to Augustus* (1737) with Horace's Epistle 1, Book II, marking the parallels, the effect is not one of passive dependency on the Latin text but of a creative adaptation of Horace's substance to Pope's satirical purposes. Something new has been made.

No carbon copy, a proper imitation, as Dryden defined it, bound a poet to keep neither to the words nor the sense of his original, "but only to set him as a pattern, and to write, as he supposes that author would have done, had he lived in our age, and in our country." The final clause of this definition certainly implies no mean imaginative ability. Imitation was a broad term. One form of it was translation, which the Augustan poets thought of as involving, like all imitation, a vying with the master. (The poetics of this special form was laid down in the Earl of Roscommon's *Essay on Translated Verse*.) Thwarted in their ambition to emulate the classical epics by that bolder kind of imitation at which only Milton had succeeded, Dryden and Pope produced translations of them instead. But it should be noted that these translations are quasi-original compositions, in which the imitator has pitted his own inventiveness against his author's. Some of the subscribers who so willingly paid the high price the booksellers demanded for Pope's *Iliad* may have thought they were purchasing Homer, as in a sense they doubtless were; but what all of them certainly got was Pope, and very memorable Pope at that. When Dr. Johnson, in his biography of the poet, referred to that work as a "poetical wonder . . . a performance which no age or nation can pretend to equal," his tribute was evoked by something bespeaking a rarer order of literary artistry than is required to produce what we now think of as a fine poetic translation. Dr. Johnson was not prodigal of laudatory superlatives. Nor is there any reason to suppose that Dryden was indulging in hyperbole in the Preface to *Sylvae* (1685), where he laid it down that to be a thorough translator a man needed to be a thorough poet. If he and Johnson could speak in such terms of the translator's art, it is easy to conceive that the more original kinds of imitation lay well outside the range of second-rate talents. And surely if imitating models had meant the sort of uninspired and mechanical copying that such historians of literary criticism as George Saintsbury and J. W. H. Atkins seemed to think, there would not be the frequent charges of plagiarism we encounter in neo-classical critical writing.

But imitation theory is not fully understood apart from the theory of genres. Hallowed by classical Greek and Roman and Italian Renaissance theorists, the idea that poetry was properly divisible into a hierarchy of kinds persisted till the dawn of romanticism. Thereafter, interest in genres declined with the virtual reduction of poetry to the lyric mode. Though Coleridge still used *epic, tragedy,* and *elegy* as terms indicative of some real if not very important distinctions of form or function, by the end of the nineteenth century the influential aesthetician Benedetto Croce was teaching the next generation of critics to regard the concept of genres as utterly devoid of aesthetic significance. In recent years, however, it has attracted renewed interest and respect, witness the spate of books on the "idea" of tragedy, the "art" of the short story, and so forth.

Their belief in the efficacy of genres profoundly influenced the way in which neoclassical critics thought of literary mimesis, and of the aims of instruction and pleasure, as well as the doctrine of imitating models. The separation of literary kinds amounts to a kind of "partitioning of mimesis," as a recent commentator[2] aptly phrases it, a recognition that there are appropriate forms for the verbal representation of prince or commoner, heroic enterprise or humble experience. And as the double aim of all literature was to delight and edify, so there was a special kind of lesson and a restricted kind of pleasure appropriate to epic, other kinds to tragedy, and yet others to each lesser genre and subgenre. Here again is glimpsed the unmistakable utilitarian bias of the neoclassical aesthetic. One doesn't drive screws with a monkey wrench. Boileau had sagely echoed Aristotle in saying as much: "Tout poème est brillant de sa propre beauté"— Every poem shines with its own peculiar beauty; and it more or less followed from this that the kinds should never be mixed. Justifying "mongrel" tragi-comedy was among the more ungrateful tasks faced by the English Augustans, one generally undertaken with an uneasy critical conscience and indifferent success.

English critics seem never to have felt it necessary to settle definitely the canon of the kinds. From time to time someone—like Hobbes, who identified six—would offer what purported to be the total list. But other critics seemed unimpressed. Still, there was a generally accepted hierarchy headed by epic and tragedy and including comedy, satire, pastoral, and lyric. As is obvious from these names the basis of distinction was haphazard and inconsistent, in one case a formal characteristic (dramatic or narrative), in another subject matter (rural life), with resulting overlappings, as between lyric and pastoral. There was considerable debate as to whether new genres might be admitted or those inherited from antiquity legitimately altered to accommodate modern tastes and conditions. Many were reluctant to think so. Edward Phillips compared the idea of a new literary genre to that of a new order in architecture, as things equally unthinkable. Dryden believed Homer had fixed forever the form of the epic poem, and in his *Discourse Concerning Satire* passed summary judgment on the epic efforts of Ariosto, Tasso, Spenser, and Milton as measured by the Homero-Virgilian standard.

Soon however, fresh and original handling of established types and the appearance of new literary and dramatic forms like opera and the novel forced critics to reexamine the categories of genre in an effort to accommodate (or to condemn) the new and different. Thus Dryden sketches the idea of opera; Addison redefines the pastoral; so does Thomas Purney in his *Full Enquiry into the True Nature of Pastoral* (1717). It is difficult, however, to trace any steady "liberalization," let alone any breakdown, of genre theory during the eighteenth century. The general reluctance to admit the legitimacy of any categories unmentioned by the ancients is reflected in the tendency to christen hitherto unknown types by graceless hyphenations of the classical nomenclature. Thus "tragi-comic," or "heroi-comic" (for Pope's *Rape*), or Fielding's "comic epic poem in prose" (for his novels). This conservatism was of course quite consistent with the prevailing view that the genres were creations neither of individual ingenuity nor of momentary social forces, but entities founded in reason and nature.* It was in fact this conception of their nature that sanctioned their indispensable function as vehicles of mimesis.

Alternative conceptions were, true enough, advanced. The growing interest in literary history during the eighteenth century was bound to show how far genres were products of historical conditions. In his *History of English*

---

* This view did not die with the eighteenth century. "We may rely upon it that we shall not improve upon the classification adopted by the Greeks for kinds of poetry," wrote Matthew Arnold in the second series of *Essays in Criticism*, "that their categories of epic, dramatic, lyric, and so forth, have a natural propriety, and should be adhered to."

Poetry (1774–1781), Thomas Warton wrote that satire was the poetry of a nation "highly polished." Thomas Blackwell's insight into the nexus between the epic and social conditions was mentioned above. The widespread desire and failure of French and English writers to produce successful epic poetry led others to similar conclusions. Certain French critics began to suspect that this most sublime of the kinds was dependent on a suitable national temperament. According to the anecdote recorded in Thomas Warton's *Observations on the Faerie Queene* (1754), Nicolas de Malézieu, after hearing Voltaire read his *Henriade,* told the author it could not succeed because "Frenchmen have no head for the epic." And Voltaire himself came to ascribe French failure in the epic form to his countrymen's being the least poetic of all civilized peoples. The status of genre implied by remarks such as these contrasts with that underlying the once common belief, expressed by Sir Richard Blackmore among many others, that English poets were unable to write an epic only because they refused to abide by the rules of the genre as laid down by Aristotle, Le Bossu, Rapin, and Dacier.

Yet the historical approach could not entirely dispel the feeling that genres, however responsive to momentary forces, essentially transcended temporal and local conditions. Though in 1766 Richard Hurd looked beyond genre distinctions to write an essay *On the Idea of Universal Poetry,* he still insisted that the pleasure afforded by any given poem was relevant to its kind. No blind reactionary on the subject, Hurd had in an earlier dissertation *On the Provinces of the Drama* (1753), accepted the "weeping comedy" and even admitted that the "mixed drama" could give delight, though of a kind reduced in proportion to the mixture. Yet these concessions do not lead him to adopt the position that genres are arbitrary. Specifically rejecting this position, in the *Universal Poetry* he considered them so far founded "in reason and the nature of things, that it will not be allowed us to multiply, or vary them, at pleasure." They may, at need, be combined, but a "true genius" will avoid doing so. Over twenty years after the success of George Lillo's *The London Merchant,* Hurd is still unwilling to grant tragic status to any play in which the action is not important and the characters not great and illustrious.

If, like Hurd and his contemporaries, one thinks of the genres as so many mimetic modes, his view is not implausible. *How* a poet imitated depended on *what* he imitated; and the willingness of eighteenth-century critics to follow classical examples owes much to their conviction that the Greeks and Romans had in fact achieved as perfect an adjustment of the *what* and the *how* as it was possible to imagine. We can more readily sympathize with their attitude if we realize that the genres are phenomena of literary form. They are, perhaps, instances of form become conventionalized, like the sonnet, that most perdurable of verse genres. So the neoclassical critic's requirement that the poet treat only tragic material in a tragic way amounts in effect to an insistence that form and content are mutually determinant, not arbitrary, an idea that has become a staple of modern poetics. But to understand and allow the validity of the theory is not necessarily to agree with any specific judgment made in its name or even to accept the terms in which it was sometimes formulated. We may be quite willing to call Lillo's play a tragedy. And surely we shall feel free to object, with Dr. Johnson in *Rambler* 125, that social class is not of itself a proper mark of genre. If absurd and despicable things are spoken and done on the stage, he wrote, the result will be comedy though it is royal persons who speak and do them. It is only necessary to remember that no more than Hurd or anyone else did Johnson mean to deny the inherent correspondence of the *what* and the *how.* He himself objected in *Rambler* 140 that Milton's reference to certain trivial objects in *Samson Agonistes* was unsuited to "a species of composition which ought to be always awful. . . ."

In effect the neoclassical writer was obliged to a double allegiance, bound in his mimesis to be faithful on the one hand to the norms and probabilities of real life and on the other to the rules and decora of the genre in which he worked. Women killed men in real life, but not, Rymer taught, in a tragedy. Dryden can lean on Le Bossu to argue, in *The Grounds of Criticism in Tragedy,* that if a prince in history had an "unprincely" fault (he mentions one who was covetous), he was "no fit person to be represented in tragedy," unless the fault were suppressed by the playwright. Pope's quarrel with Ambrose Philips, his rival in pastoral verse, involved this same tension between the demands of reality and the requirements of the genre. Philips favored a close imitation of rustic manners and speech whereas Pope thought a more "artful" image of rural life preferable. The most refined taste then favored Pope, as John Hughes, an early editor of Spenser, realized. In the *Shepherd's Calendar,* Hughes admitted, some readers will find "too much of the *merum rus* [pure rustic]." In these arguments we meet again the principle to which Dryden made telling appeal in his retort to Howard, that if blank verse was nearer to nature, rhyme was nearer the nature of tragedy. Genres, it is plain, were powerful deterrents to literary naturalism in neoclassical times.

But if they were thus indispensable vehicles of mimesis as neoclassical critics conceived of it, they were intimately involved as well in the process of imitating models. One imitated *within,* and according to the laws of, a given kind. When an especially daring soul resolved to outdo the masterpiece he had taken for his model, it often meant that he was able to see *in the genre itself* possibilities which the older poet had neglected to exploit. The hierarchy of the kinds was sometimes also thought of as a poetic *gradus ad Parnassum.* The neophyte (Milton and Pope are examples) began by serving an apprenticeship to love lyric or pastoral, graduating later to epic or the greater didactic forms. His choice of models was a similar process: he might first try his hand at something in the manner of Ovid or of an esteemed modern, Cowley or Waller, before daring to contend with Homer, Virgil, or Shakespeare for epic or tragic honors.

NATURE'S FAITHFUL COPIERS

The abiding love for the ancient classics, the belief in a great literary tradition, and the faith in the efficacy of the genres are in some sort premises from which the idea of imitating masterpieces looks more like a quite logical inference than an absurd maxim by which the otherwise sensible men of the Age of Reason were mysteriously bemused. Seen in isolation, however, as a piece of practical advice, the injunction that an author pattern his work on someone else's is difficult to understand or defend. This is why readers are embarrassed to find a man like Dryden applying the terms "judicious" and "learned" to Thomas Rymer, who in his *Short View of Tragedy* furnished an elaborate example of such advice. In that book, in the damning company of his notorious attack on Shakespeare's *Othello* as "a bloody farce," Rymer soberly outlined and recommended to Dryden a plot for a tragedy on the Spanish Armada modeled on that of Aeschylus' *The Persians*. What he proposed seems hardly the right approach to imitation: Aeschylus' tight unities of time and place are to be exactly kept; in place of Darius' tomb the scene is to be a drawing-room in the palace at Madrid; fifteen grandees of Spain will replace Aeschylus' fifteen Persian elders as chorus. In its main line of action the play is to be almost a replica of the Aeschylean plot. News of the Armada's destruction will ironically supervene upon eager expectations of easy victory over England, as in the Greek play Xerxes' supposedly invincible fleets and armies meet humiliating defeat in their expedition against the Greeks. Then, lest the moral of all this be missed, the chorus is to close its final ode of lamentation with a *sententia* lifted from Euripides: "Thus you see the Gods bring things to pass often, otherwise than was by man proposed," as Rymer lamely renders it. This doesn't seem to be the way Dryden had used Shakespeare's *Antony and Cleopatra* as his guide in the composition of *All for Love*, still less the means by which Pope nourished his satiric genius by the example of Horace, or Dr. Johnson took inspiration from Juvenal for his *London*.

Yet Rymer's scheme is by no means absurd. Perhaps only if a playwright of known ability had attempted to carry it out, and failed, could we be sure that here was one of those miserable instances of copying the *Iliad* instead of Homer. But that is the chief thing to remember about imitation: more than any other tenet of neoclassical literary theory, it can be neither justified nor understood apart from the practice to which it was put by the most gifted writers of the time.

Part of the reason for this is that the rationale of model-imitation, like the theory of genres, was never fully elaborated even by its warmest eighteenth-century advocates. Their failure to do so has resulted not only in the purblind denigration of the idea by Saintsbury and lesser scholars, but in a failure to appreciate its central importance in neoclassical literary thought and art. What neoclassical theorists did say in its behalf usually seems to be something not worth being taken very seriously, such as the notion that human experience and capacity being limited, a poet's job consists principally in the effort to do what has already been done, with the hope, it may be, of doing it better and the obligation of doing it differently. It hardly needs saying that the nineteenth century had little patience with this belief, and many people today still cannot see what there is to justify it. The general supposition has therefore been that it was an attitude historically generated, brought about by something peculiar to the all-too-circumscribed intellectual horizons in which the Drydens and Johnsons were fated to do their thinking. But while the historian of ideas is carefully documenting this thesis, someone else may be pondering some lines written by a twentieth-century poet whose work was original to the point of being called revolutionary. In *East Coker* T. S. Eliot envisages the poet's labor of creation with a modesty at once disarming and arresting:

> And what there is to conquer
> By strength and submission, has already been discovered
> Once or twice, or several times, by men whom one cannot hope
> To emulate—but there is no competition—
> There is only the fight to recover what has been lost
> And found and lost again and again: and now, under conditions
> That seem unpropitious.[3]

It's a fair guess that Dante, whose *Divine Comedy* Eliot briefly and deftly imitates elsewhere in *Four Quartets,* was among those he considered beyond emulation. For Addison's contemporaries it would have been Virgil. But despite even profounder differences that separate two contrasting historical periods, Eliot's measured confession of the burden and challenge with which the literary past confronts a modern poet can suggest a new and more sympathetic angle of vision on the neoclassical writer's preoccupation with some great exemplar of the tradition at the very moment when he was struggling to make his own contribution.

If it is true that the neoclassical critics put the case for imitation badly, it should be said in palliation that the issues involved are remarkably complex. Where, for example, is the line to be drawn between a proper imitation and plagiarism? In no other period of literary history, be it noted, have charges of plagiarism been more frequent. Gerard Langbaine, whom Dr. Johnson dubbed "the great detector of plagiarism," included in his *Account of the English Dramatick Poets* (1691) an ill-tempered "exposé" of what he called Dryden's thefts from other playwrights, while praising Ben Jonson's "imitations." English critics followed the French in likening a plagiarist to a petty thief, a successful imitator to a great conqueror. Dryden himself pictured Ben Jonson as "invading" ancient works and grandly making them his own. There is no doubt, however, that in the hands of poetasters the imitative process was often no more than a cover for literary pilferage, with the result that imitation itself came into bad odor. In 1751 Hurd published with his edition of Horace's *Epistola ad Augustum* a discourse entitled *On Poetical Imitation,* followed in 1757 by a letter to William Mason *On the Marks of Imitation.* In these he tried to clear the air by defending imitation itself and distinguishing the use from the abuse by citing examples.

The intricacies of the problem are revealed in the tendency of some critics to self-contradiction and uncertainty in what they say about it. It is the more superficial thinkers who by facile simplification offer the most unequivocal opinions. Typical of these is the anonymous author of *An Essay on the New Species of Writing* (1751), who flatly condemns imitations of any kind on the grounds that every writer is a unique personality. To the more thoughtful it was clear that the matter was not so simple, as Dryden perceived when in *A Parallel of Poetry and Painting* he wrote that an imitator without invention was only a plagiarist, yet (in the same paragraph) that to copy the best models was a laudable practice: in fact, "a copy after Raphael is more to be commended than an original of any indifferent painter." Since both statements can be easily defended, the paradox must be only apparent or partial. The first step toward a possible resolution is not only to separate servile from creative imitation, petty theft from conquest, but also to discover what it is that makes the difference, a far more exacting affair. Why is it that an obviously unoriginal writer is distasteful to the extent that his work betrays its similarity to another's, while Pope and Milton are actually enriched for readers who become aware of the earlier works on which they drew? * To compound the puzzle, are there not also borderline cases which one critic may praise as traditional and another blame as derivative? Even Dr. Johnson was uncertain whether some of Dryden's comedies were indifferently successful imitations or downright plagiarisms.

Years earlier he had tried to clarify the difference in one of the most interesting of the *Rambler* papers, number 143. The charge of plagiarism, he decided, was justified only in cases where ideas originally expressed elsewhere are joined in a new poem without "necessary coherence," or else where the words as well as the thought have been copied. Among examples of the latter fault he offers Pope's borrowing from Richard Crashaw for the opening lines of his epitaph on Elijah Fenton:

> *This modest stone, what few vain marbles can,*
> *May truly say, Here lies an honest man.*

Crashaw's version had run:

> *. . . this plain floor*
> *Believe me, reader, can say more*
> *Than many a braver marble can,*
> *Here lies a truly honest man.*

But the baffling nature of the whole imitation-plagiarism question can be illustrated from this very example. May a reader not legitimately conclude Pope's tight couplet to be an improvement on Crashaw's more diffuse quatrain?

Anyone who wished to supply a satisfactory answer to this question would find himself forced into a re-examination of the ideas of convention and genre and of the intricate relation between tradition and individual talent—an inquiry beyond the scope of this book. Cer-

---

* "Milton," William Hazlitt declared in his *Lectures on the English Poets*, "has borrowed more than any other writer, and exhausted every source of imitation, sacred or profane; yet he is perfectly distinct from every other writer. He is a writer of centos, and yet in originality scarcely inferior to Homer."

tainly the literary critics of the Enlightenment were ill-equipped to undertake so profound an investigation. Nonetheless, one manifestation of the enduring value of their speculations can be seen in the fact that certain neoclassical insights into literary imitation take on fresh cogency and suggestiveness in the light of what twentieth-century theorists have recently been saying about the place and function of conventions and genres in literature.

To those who, like the author of the *Essay on the New Species of Writing* just mentioned, cried up originality by appealing to the uniqueness of each creative personality, other critics opposed a more inclusive analogy. Although a poem undoubtedly reflects the human uniqueness of the man who wrote it, it is a uniqueness within a recognizable kinship to his ancestors. "Therefore," wrote Pope in the 1717 Preface to his *Works,* "they who say our thoughts are not our own, because they resemble the Ancients, may as well say our faces are not our own, because they are like our Fathers. . . ." Like Pope here, Dryden and other poets envisaged the tradition as a poetic genealogy and felt themselves to be scions of a noble ancestry. The best known instance of this metaphor is the wish Pope versified in the *Essay on Criticism* that some spark of the ancient bards' celestial fire might "The last, the meanest of your sons inspire." Though analogies never prove anything they are often effective weapons for exposing error or half-truth, this one especially so. It dramatizes that the logical end of demanding originality above all must be the production of new works that in their radical dissimilarity to the old would be monsters, just as a child too individualized would be a freak. And by the same token both work and child would be hideous.

On the other hand, the injunction to compose with one eye on some celebrated model in the same genre is admittedly something less than satisfactory and almost calculated to induce the creative follies to which it gave rise in seventeenth- and eighteenth-century France and

England. But that is an old and familiar story told and retold in the standard histories of literature and of criticism, in which all that can fairly be urged against literary imitation—and much that cannot—is duly recorded. In recent years, scholars freed of the romanticist bias under which the writers of those histories labored have done much to redress the balance of estimate, though not enough, I think, to dispel the image of eighteenth-century proponents of originality in heroic defiance of a stodgy and wrong-headed traditionalism.

That this impression should die hard is not surprising when one notices that the very vocabulary of the debate makes heavily, especially in modern ears, for the case against imitation. Who today, if ever, can be against originality, freedom, self-reliance, genius? But the gist of the argument of those who in the names of these ideals decried the whole doctrine of imitation wants scanning. Starting from the quite reasonable position that Homer and Nature (*pace* Pope) were *not* the same, they moved to the more questionable one that Homer might come between the poet and Nature, obscuring his view, and from there to the quite unreasonable conclusion that Nature could be captured only in total disregard of Homer. "Go to life, not to books." The validity of this conclusion is belied by literary history, which not alone for the neoclassical era but virtually from the beginning to the present tells of writers learning or even receiving their vocation from the example of older writers. Knowing this to be true, the neoclassical advocates of imitation were additionally aware—some of them doubtless by introspection of their own artistic growth—that the imagination is educated, primarily if not exclusively, through the study of its own best products. Sensitive minds have often since confirmed their insight. Prophet though he was of self-reliance in letters as in conduct, Ralph Waldo Emerson wrote that it is chiefly books that speak to the imagination; that "only poetry inspires poetry."

Echoed by men of limited intelligence, this idea was often so ineptly represented during the eighteenth century as to deafen the ears of many people to the earnest pleas of those who were urging young poets to immerse themselves in the classics. It is not hard to see why no person of talent or taste could put much stock in this advice after Samuel Wesley had commended the example of Sir Richard Blackmore's unreadable epics. "Each page," sang Wesley in an *Epistle to a Friend Concerning Poetry* (1700),

> *is big with Virgil's Manly thought,*
> *To follow him too near's a glorious Fault.*

Critical infatuation of this kind is what has made it easy for some students of the neoclassical aesthetic to dismiss the very idea of model-imitation as insensate nonsense. There precisely, they have said, is the inevitable result of it, a Blackmore!

It now seems odd not to have noticed, however, that such was not always the result. Where Blackmore failed, Milton triumphed; and if Wesley was obtuse, Addison was perceptive. It was in *Spectator* 333, one of eighteen devoted to an analysis of *Paradise Lost,* that Addison relished the echoes of the *Iliad* and the *Aeneid* that he detected in Milton's description of the war in Heaven. The revered Longinus, he recalled, had taught that a poet about to write on a given topic ought to try to imagine how Homer would have treated it. "By this Means," Addison observed, "one great Genius often catches the Flame from another, and writes in his Spirit without copying servilely after him." But not even the philosophically inclined Spectator felt any need to probe the causes and conditions of this admirable contagion, perhaps because when he wrote, it had long enjoyed massive critical support and not yet been subjected to serious question.

Reasoned defenses of literary imitation arose in response to later challenges from the spokesmen for originality. The best of these defenses was Richard Hurd's essay *On Poetical Imitation* already mentioned. In arresting anticipation of twentieth-century conceptions of the mimetic process, Hurd argued first that in point of fact no one can grasp the living forms of nature immediately and directly. Even the strongest inventive talent views reality to some extent through the eyes of the poets he has read. Indeed, it is they who teach him *how* to see, as Reynolds was also to say later on in the eleventh of his *Discourses on Art*. The imitation of models is in this sense propaedeutic to the imitation of nature. Hurd insists on this point even while admitting that too much reading may on occasion stifle creativity, as he believes to have been the case with Addison's poetry. One passage of *On Poetical Imitation* is remarkable for its affinity to modern theories of convention and archetype. Hurd detected "fixed and real analogies between different *material objects;* between these objects and the *inward workings* of the mind; and, again, between these, and the *external signs* of them." Since, he reasons, a poet is forced to think of these analogies without deliberately searching for them, they suffice of themselves to explain the frequent parallels between writers who could not have known each other's work: those between Homer and the Bible for example.

So far, this line of reasoning only enforces an ineluctable limit to originality by positing that all literature is essentially conventional. But some neoclassical poets and critics made even bolder claims for imitation. Under the best conditions they conceived it to be a positive aid to successful composition and not the hindrance it was often represented to be. Dryden believed that by imitating Shakespeare in the composition of *All for Love* he had excelled himself, a judgment largely confirmed by comparing that tragedy to his others. Many writers noticed that a heightened creative fertility seemed to ensue from what Pope called the "mutual commerce" of two minds. In a letter written to Walsh in 1706 he compared one poet's borrowing from another to the process of grafting shoots on fruit trees to make them produce in greater variety. "A mutual commerce makes poetry flourish." This is why, as Hurd also perceived, a good imitation often excels its model and has about it no air of the factitious, of being a fabrication at second hand. Thomas Gray wrote to Horace Walpole in 1748 that the poem *London,* Dr. Johnson's satire in imitation of Juvenal, was "one of those few imitations that have all the spirit of an original." Although Gray seems to have been agreeably mystified, others, like Reynolds, came to believe that the valued quality men call originality is, precisely if paradoxically, the result of the right kind of imitating.

Recent speculation suggests that this paradox too is an illusion. In an essay happily entitled *Nature and Homer,* Northrop Frye challenges the idea that life or experience can ever be the "formal" cause of art, because "the impulse to give a literary shape to something can only come from previous contact with literature." All literature being thus "derivative," the truly original work, Frye concludes, is only "derivative at a deeper level." [4] In *Anatomy of Criticism* he argues that the difference between the original and the imitative poet is "simply that the former is more profoundly imitative." His most provocative generalization, that originality "returns to the origins of literature, as radicalism returns to its roots," [5] immediately recalls Eliot's editorial remark in *The Criterion* for April, 1924, that though classicism is in a sense reactionary, "it must be in a profounder sense revolutionary." Eliot and Frye may be only dramatically overstating the peculiar effect of perennial freshness that a great traditional literary work has on readers. Perhaps Sainte-Beuve was nearer the mark in his belief that the true classic could at first *appear* revolutionary because it is at once old and new, therefore forever up-to-date.

In any case, in ascribing this rare quality of unfading originality to a more profound imitation, Frye provides a sounder *apologia* for the neoclassic doctrine than the eighteenth-century critics themselves were in any position to do. Without adopting the particular categories of genre, style, and technique that made up the conventions of literature as they knew them, it restores the idea of literary convention itself to something like the position it held in neoclassic theory. We begin to see the point of the Augustan faith in the imitation of masterpieces and the validity of genres when we begin to think of conventions as something inherent in literature and inseparable from it, and not merely as adventitious characteristics of certain more or less archaic forms like classical epic or medieval romance. Inescapably, acceptance of this idea entails consequences which some modern social and educational theorists might find alarming. Like neoclassical imitation doctrine, these recent concepts of the conventionality of literature imply a certain minimal education on the part of both author and reader. The sense of convention that liberates a writer's creative powers and enriches a reader's appreciation can be attained only by knowing literature itself, and it is best attained by knowing the best literature. In *Anatomy of Criticism* Frye admits that he has in mind the cultivated reader, and he traces the decline of respect for conventions and archetypes to "a deficiency in contemporary education." [6] However this may be, anyone reading the neoclassical literary critics today does well to keep in mind that for them humanistic learning, the more of it the better, was indispensable to author or critic. Cowley, Dr. Johnson was glad to record in *The Lives of the English Poets,* was favored by great learning, his verse "embellished with all the ornaments which books could supply. . . ." Pope alludes often and with ill-veiled self-esteem to his own studies and occasionally praises the learning of other poets and critics. It was as much a truism in his day as it is now that the delights of letters are accessible only to the reasonably literate; but reasonable literacy was then understood to involve much more than the bare ability to decipher script.

If we are better prepared today than were scholars of

a generation ago to assess the neoclassical critic's concern with literary conventions of every kind—with genres, with rhyme, with certain verse and stanza forms—it is because we have made our own rediscovery of a truth they took for granted and the poetics of vulgarized romanticism mistook for heresy. Increasingly, critical thought is coming to see that conventions are not clogs but aids to the creative imagination. But this idea must not be misconstrued. It does not mean that a writer may by conscious choice avail himself of this or that established form or technique as a handy labor-saving vehicle or container by which to convey or embody what he has first invented. It is not surprising that preromantic English critics themselves should often have been guilty of this misconception since it so naturally follows from the creative theory of Le Bossu, who had persuaded them that a poet first decides on a moral or theme and then finds a form appropriate to its expression. In the light of more satisfactory views of artistic creation (ultimately derived, ironically, from romantic theory), it is now apparent that conventions themselves are heuristic, allowing a writer to conceive or discover values and significances his unaided genius would never have come upon. The chapter on *Conventions and the Individual Talent* in Paul Fussell's *Poetic Meter and Poetic Form*,[7] to name only the most recent of such affirmations, adds weight to Dryden's remark in the Preface to *The Rival Ladies* that rhyme can bring forth "the richest and clearest thoughts." Dryden had obviously glimpsed in rhyme what a poet-critic of our day and country, John Crowe Ransom, discovered in meter, "a powerful intellectual determinant." [8]

The danger, of course, which spokesmen for originality rightly saw, lay in using conventions as a substitute for creative effort. Nonetheless, this was a danger to which the ablest defenders of traditionalism were equally alert. Pope himself devoted a chapter of *Peri Bathous* to satirizing the delusions of those who believed an epic poem could be composed by recipe. What is not so apparent to the uninstructed common sense of any period is the folly of the opposite extreme. Richard Hurd was among those alive to the consequences of a determination to be original at all costs: "an awkward straining," as he calls it in the essay on *Poetical Imitation*, destructive of all grace and beauty. He holds up Davenant's dreary heroic poem *Gondibert* as an inevitable product of the tradition-defying attitude voiced in its Preface. Davenant might have taken warning from the fate of Statius, who in order to show his originality was careful to make the funeral games of his *Thebiad* different from those of Homer and Virgil. The result was total failure because, Hurd explains, "impossible it is, without deserting nature herself, to dissent from her faithful copiers. . . ." * Reynolds was later to deliver the same opinion in his *Discourses* before the Royal Academy. As so often happened in his day, Hurd's way of putting it is not entirely persuasive. The modern conception of tradition and convention more plausibly suggests that if a writer has acquired that awareness of his literary ancestry which T. S. Eliot and neo-classical imitation theorists alike considered requisite to successful composition, his work is bound to resemble that produced by nature's other faithful copiers. Under these circumstances his best course is to shun both deliberate dissent and deliberate conformity. Whatever their differences in formulation, however, the net effect of recent investigation is to confirm as a sound corollary of the imitation theory the axiom that a conscious aim to be different exposes a writer to the risk of artistic barrenness.

* Pope's creative imitation of Greek, Latin, and English poetic models has been thoroughly analyzed in Reuben Arthur Brower's *Alexander Pope: The Poetry of Allusion* (Oxford, 1959). Professor Brower's final sentence deserves emphasis: "For Pope at the start of his career, as at the end, the imitation of life is also the imitation of literature" (p. 361).

V *SAMUEL JOHNSON*

SOME PRELIMINARY OBSERVATIONS

Although students of literary criticism have not hesitated to name Samuel Johnson as the leading English critic of his century, they have been hard put to it to justify the nomination. As J. W. H. Atkins noted, they have felt constrained to do so apologetically. George Saintsbury's hedging declaration, "But, as he is, he is great," sums up the equivocal judgment usually rendered on Johnson's achievement, in which what has to be conceded or excused sometimes threatens to outweigh the favorable evidence. Nor have his commentators been in very close accord as to what to admire and what to deplore. Johnson's *Preface to Shakespeare* (1765), which was for Saintsbury marred by exasperating contradictions, Nichol Smith found unsurpassable as a "balanced estimate" of the great playwright. Where Johnsonians do agree, in more general praise, it is directed to qualities for which some of Johnson's predecessors and contemporaries are equally preeminent. Those who cry up a classical, "Augustan" Johnson have to admit that he is less so, or less purely so, than Addison or Pope or even Dennis. Those who applaud rather a liberal, anti-Augustan Johnson are uncomfortably aware that in many respects the critical writings of the Warton brothers and Hurd constitute a more effective and constructive critique of moribund critical rationalism than anything that can be found in Johnson. Whatever may have pleased his readers from time to time, the significant fact is that Johnson the critic continues to have detractors less readily controvertible than those encountered by Johnson the poet, the arch-Tory, the moralist.

And yet he survives. The causes and conditions of this survival ought therefore most satisfactorily to define whatever it is that gives his critical writings their enduring value. Remarkably, even after both assenting to the most damaging censures of Johnson's criticism and rejecting outright some of the claims made for it, one can return to the Shakespeare *Preface* or the *Lives of the Poets* with no sense that their interest, their interest *as literary criticism,* has been diminished. Professor René Wellek, for example, devotes much of his chapter on Johnson in *A History of Modern Criticism* to documenting the charges that he hardly understood the nature of art, that he confused it with life and ultimately made it superfluous, "a mere vehicle for the communication of moral or psychological truth." [1] Assuming Wellek's charges to be justified, as I think they very largely are, it is hard to imagine an indictment more destructive to the reputation of a literary critic. Since their import is to convict Johnson of a serious deficiency in literary theory, it is sensible to conclude that his claim to our respect lies elsewhere, in some innovation of judgment or excellence of practical technique. But it is precisely here that the modern student finds several venerable red herrings dragged across the path of his investigation. Though the specialists—or some of them—will have long since recognized these for what they are, less informed readers may need to be alerted to the more specious of them. Most notable is the heresy that in the *Preface to Shakespeare* Johnson put an end once and for all to the dramatic unities of time and place, whereas in fact his reasoning was neither new nor universally convincing. This heresy is part of a more general misconception that Johnson somehow destroyed neoclassicism itself and so prepared the way for romanticism. Although the main instigator of this notion, Saintsbury, is now a somewhat discredited authority, it has enough surface plausibility to justify examining how a minor truth has been made to propagate a major error.

The minor truth is that like other Englishmen before him Johnson thought some of the literary rules were arbitrary and absurd, others well founded. It is also true that he knew how to say so memorably, as in the much quoted section of *Rambler* 156:

> It ought to be the first endeavour of a writer to distinguish nature from custom, or that which is established because it is right from that which is right only because it is established, that he may neither violate essential principles by a desire of novelty nor debar himself from the attainment of beauties within his view by a needless fear of breaking rules which no literary dictator had authority to enact.

"With this utterance, this single utterance," runs a sentence of Saintsbury's, "all the ruling doctrines of sixteenth, seventeenth, and eighteenth century criticism received notice to quit." [2] If this sentence is not patent nonsense it is hard to know what it can mean. In the first place Johnson himself openly subscribed to most of what are usually and rightly taken to be "the ruling doctrines" of neoclassicism, though he preferred to interpret them in his own terms. Among them are the doctrines that art imitates nature, that its end is to instruct and delight, that its norm and arbiter are truth and nature, the probable and the universal. The more one reads Johnson's prose the less reason there is to doubt that these broad governing principles were those he considered to be natural and essential. There is even less reason for wondering what he had in mind when he spoke of "rules which no literary dictator had authority to enact," because he gives a few samples in this very *Rambler*: that no more than three actors should be on stage at once, that a play must have five acts, that comic and tragic materials should never be mixed. From his other writings we know that he also classed the time and place unities among rules based merely on custom and arbitrary edict, whereas, again from *Rambler* 156, we know that he considered the unity of action to be a rule "fixed and obligatory."

Anyone who has read through a decent anthology of English literary criticism with even moderate attention will recognize at once that what Johnson condemns here is what most major critics in England had been condemning since Dryden's earliest prefaces. His "single utterance" recasts a familiar argument into the kind of telling abstractions that came so readily to his generalizing mind. But he is original neither in refusing to accept critical authority nor in insisting that a writer ought to distinguish the natural from the customary. Addison was at least as daring when in similar vein he announced in *Spectator* 273 his intention of commenting on Aristotle's rules as well as on Milton's epic; and when later, in *Spectator* 321, he asserted his right not only to pick and choose among the rules laid down by the recognized critics of the epic, but even "sometimes to differ from all of them, when I have thought that the Reason of the Thing was on my side." This was precisely what, following Dryden's precept and example, he proceeded to do. Addison, we can assume, was among those who emboldened Johnson to say in the *Lives of the Poets* that "reason wants not Horace to support it." If like Atkins we accept Saintsbury's judgment that Johnson's memorable pronouncement sounded the death knell of the neoclassical system we are forced to the grotesque conclusion that in England neoclassicism's funeral bells began to toll at the hour of its birth. The confusion induced by this line of thought becomes apparent when Atkins in a single paragraph declares that Johnson was "no adherent of the neo-classical school" and that he "renews in a more determined form the challenge of Addison and the rest" [3] to its doctrines. Poor English neoclassicism—if Johnson, Addison, and "the rest" were its enemies, who were its spokesmen?

Proponents of a preromantic Johnson have pointed to the use made of him by a French apostle of romanticism, Stendhal, who enlisted the renowned Englishman in his cause by publishing a free translation of the attack on the unities from the *Preface to Shakespeare*. Yet because Johnson could be polemically effective in helping to batter down the Bastille of rigid French classicism, it does not follow that he was an enemy to the literary system that had prevailed in England from Dryden's time to his own. On the contrary, the whole tendency of his critical theory and practice, and his literary taste, amply supports Professor Walter Bate's judgment that Johnson is in fact "the greatest critical exponent of English neo-classicism,"[4] his very reservations and misgivings about some of its restrictions being themselves grounded in neoclassical doctrines.

Modern scholarship has quite effectively exposed the romantic Johnson as a historical fiction. Unfortunately, certain other claims made on his behalf, not in themselves total misinterpretations so much as interpretative misfocusings, continue to obscure our view of what constitutes Johnson's distinctive importance as a critic. We have been told that among his major contributions to theory is the test of time. The final criterion of worth, he is fond of repeating, is how long a literary work continues to be read and admired. But this is no more than a truism that evades the question of literary excellence by posing it anew. What causes one work to appeal through the ages and another to be forgotten is the very problem any respectable theory of value seeks to solve. Or again, we are bidden to admire Johnson's insistence on judging a poem as a whole, not by its parts. This claim is equally hopeless as a basis for distinction both because it was a pretty old chestnut by the time Johnson gave it his blessing and because he violated it in practice at least as often as he followed it. After speaking scornfully of those who commend Shakespeare for single passages taken out of context, he repeatedly did so himself both in the *Preface* and in his commentary on the several plays, as August von Schlegel was among the first to point out. The historical method, according to which a critic in judging a work takes into consideration the circumstances during which it was written, is another idea often credited to Johnson that he honored more by lip service than by application. "Time and place," he grandly observed, "must always enforce regard," but it is not noticeable that they often enforced *his* regard. His nearest approach to doing so is in palliating a supposed fault in a writer, as when he excused the witches in *Macbeth* by reference to the belief in sorcery and enchantment prevalent in Elizabethan England. Johnson is no historical relativist; we recognize the true tone of the man and the critic in the brusque sentence passed on what he took to be the moral indifference Shakespeare displayed toward his characters: "This fault the barbarity of his age cannot extenuate . . . justice is a virtue independent on time or place."

There is probably no knowing for certain why alone of the great critics Samuel Johnson should have suffered the bizarre fate of being praised for virtues to which others have obviously better claims. Yet a hint of the reason may be glimpsed by any discerning admirer of the *Lives* of Dryden and Pope or the *Preface to Shakespeare* who is asked to state in so many words what quality or qualities give these works their appeal. He will, I submit, find this hard to do, and therefore be in danger, if pressed, of falling back on some such generalizations as those just mentioned, confident of having explicit warrant for them in Johnson's own words. But if, having done so, he turns again to his favorite pages, he may be surprised to discover how remote they are from these considerations or indeed from anything capable of abstract formulation.

THE CRITICAL THEORY

On the other hand there is no denying that Johnson entertained a set of criteria which he deliberately applied in appraising books and authors. Subject to certain qualifications that will appear below, it is hard to resist the conclusion that no other critic before or since ever set out on his career burdened with convictions about literature more inimical on the whole to good criticism. They are the fundamental determinants of his total critical attitude and of many of his specific judgments. For good or ill they constitute the nearest thing to a consistent literary theory that can be gleaned from his writings and conversation. They therefore deserve to be identified and examined.

Before doing so, however, we need to consider the widely held view that Johnson really had no fixed critical principles but was a kind of freewheeling empiricist convinced of the futility of all theory. It should be granted at once that this view is encouraged by Johnson's own declarations. If, as he wrote in the *Preface to Shakespeare,* "there is always an appeal open from criticism to nature," then why, a reader may fairly ask, trouble with "criticism" at all, that is, with any definitions of literary value, criteria of judgment, or techniques of analysis that ever have been or ever can be formulated? The inclusive import of his opposed terms—"criticism" and "nature"— might even raise the suspicion that his distrust of critical principles does not stop at the alternative of a judicious impressionism but implies at the deepest level of his consciousness a despair of the critical activity itself. His very fondness for invoking length of esteem as the only test of literary excellence implies the vanity of critical knowledge, especially if we recall that an early reference to it, in *Rambler* 92, is prompted by a lack of agreement among the critics, each of whom is swayed in judgment by personal interests and passions. He goes here to the length of asserting that beauty in literature is an unaccountable quality, "so little subject to the examinations of reason, that *Paschal* supposes it to end where demonstration begins. . . ." An out-and-out subjective impressionist, a Jules Lemaître or an Anatole France, could hardly ask for a better confirmation of his views.

Yet in this same *Rambler* Johnson also insists that it is a critic's function "to establish principles" and to replace opinion by knowledge. He believes it a goal no less attainable than necessary to rescue criticism from the "anarchy of ignorance" and the "caprices of fancy" as well as from the "tyranny of prescription." This goal was not a momentary ideal later abandoned. One of his few consistent applications of the historical estimate appears in the *Lives of the Poets,* written in old age, where he is at pains to defend Addison against the charge of critical impressionism, of "deciding by taste rather than by principles." Given the crude state of learning at the time, Addison did the best he could. And every reader will remember that in an appreciation of Dryden's criticism that has never been surpassed Johnson honors him first and foremost for having "taught us to determine upon principles the merit of composition." From this statement it would seem to follow of necessity that principles do exist and that they can be known and communicated. This was certainly the firm belief of many in Johnson's century. Its most notable manifestation is the long line of treatises written by philosophers of the beautiful, most of them Scotsmen, that begins with Francis Hutcheson's *Inquiry into the Original of Our Ideas of Beauty and Virtue* (1725) and culminates in Archibald Alison's *Essays on the Nature and Principles of Taste* (1790). These men saw in empirical philosophy, especially in the associationism of Locke and later David Hartley, the basis for isolating and defining the mental faculties by which objects of beauty are produced and appreciated.

But Johnson was not one of them. Boswell has recorded his opinion of Lord Kames' *Elements of Criticism* (1762), one of the best and most influential of these works, which he called "a pretty essay . . . though much of it is chimerical," at best presenting old ideas in a new way. To Johnson the whole enterprise in which Kames and his countrymen were engaged was bound to appear ultimately futile. For all his references to judging by principle and to the "science" of criticism, he was profoundly skeptical of attempts to rationalize imaginative experience. Though in *Rambler* 92 he could speak with easy confidence of bringing literature "under the dominion of science," what he says elsewhere suggests this intellectual conquest to be severely limited. He begins *Rambler* 125, which exposes the inadequacy of certain definitions of comedy, by citing the legal maxim that "definitions are hazardous," something beyond the compass of the human intellect. He argues that this maxim applies equally to the domain of criticism, especially to that "licentious and vagrant faculty" the imagination, which eludes all analysis. Even to distinguish the essentials of the various genres Johnson regards as an effort foredoomed to failure, since every new genius subverts the established rules. He seems untroubled by the obvious tendency of such arguments to risk abandoning literary speculation to that very "anarchy of ignorance," which he had so recently declared it the critic's duty to resist. His advice that dramatic theorists define comedy simply as "such a dramatic representation of human life as may excite mirth," and let it go at that, certainly gives the impression that Johnson's critical science was a curiously elementary discipline.

It is possible that Johnson's self-contradictions spring from some deep-seated uncertainty as to the validity and usefulness of abstract literary principles. It is more likely though that he was voicing his truer convictions in those passages of his writings that set the pretensions of theorists at defiance. They consist better with the ruggedly empirical temper that marks virtually everything he wrote and is so unmistakable a part of his character as pictured in the biographies and memorials of those who knew him.

In addition, Johnson's general conception of literature was essentially hostile to literary and critical theory as such. Normally, a literary theory rests on the assumption that literature is something *sui generis,* though obviously related in countless ways to extraliterary thought and experience. It therefore aims to be as far as possible a unique discipline concerned with properties and issues defined and analyzed by a terminology peculiarly its own. It was not so for Johnson. For him literature was first and last an instrumentality of moral action directed always to uses and values beyond, and presumably higher, than itself. "Poetry," he wrote in the *Life of Milton,* "is the art of uniting pleasure with truth, by calling imagination to the help of reason." *How* pleasure unites with truth, or imagination collaborates with reason, and what is the mode of their agency—these are questions inevitably raised by critics who, like Coleridge for example, see the poet as fulfilling a unique role. For a critic like Johnson, for whom the poet is valued mainly as an especially beloved and effective ally of the moral philosopher, these questions are neglected not only because they seem unanswerable but also, and chiefly, because they are trivial, not worth the effort.

So, scholars have sometimes concluded, somewhat wearily, Johnson's critical method is empirical and pragmatic, one that judges books by the kind and quality of the response they elicit, not by preconceived theories of form or ideas of function belonging to literature and literature alone. And though when he wrote *Rambler* 156 Johnson thought it unwise to use the pragmatic test, to "judge works of genius merely by the event," he later did so often enough to justify describing him as an empiricist.

The one serious objection to this description is that it leaves so much out of account. It overlooks certain aspects of Johnson's habitual approach to literature that establish his commitment to the essential tenets of neoclassicism and at the same time show the modification they underwent in his powerful and highly individual mind. If Johnson declined to pass judgment by applying such purely literary rules as those enjoining a strict separation of the genres, adherence to the dramatic unities, and conventional character decorum, he was nonetheless far from open-minded. In the place of these purely literary canons he substituted three broad extraliterary or quasi-literary criteria which I shall designate by the convenient if awkward terms moralism, realism, and generality. The neoclassical provenance of these terms is obvious, but Johnson redefined and applied them according to his own philosophy and temperament.

Perhaps nothing in Samuel Johnson is so embarrassing to modern readers as his constant application of moral standards to imaginative literature. Even his staunchest admirers are in disagreement about it. According to T. S. Eliot, the edification that Johnson demands of a poem is not a detachable addition to it but an organically essential ingredient, so that the reader enjoys a single unified experience, not the two experiences of pleasure and edification separately.[5] This would be a comforting interpretation if it could be supported by the evidence of Johnson's writings. Few readers even today are put off by criticism that is morally oriented—much of the best criticism has quite properly been so—provided that it does not expect moral values in a work of literature to be overtly expressed. Yet as another of his modern admirers understands him this is what Johnson does expect. F. R. Leavis has been moved to declare flatly that "for Johnson a moral judgment that isn't *stated* isn't there."[6] There are, it should be noted, exceptions to Leavis' statement, but as a generalization about Johnson it is unfortunately sounder than Eliot's.

In Johnson's case, quite apparently, the dominant preoccupation of his age with the writer's moral function was intensified by the constitutional moralism of the man himself. He belongs in the company of the great moralists. A moralist is not someone who merely advocates a set of rules for human conduct. Nor is he merely someone skilled in exposing the disguises by which men conceal from others, and from themselves, the real motives of their behavior, though as with Pascal, La Rochefoucauld, or Johnson himself, that is usually part of his talent and aim. A moralist of Johnson's type is one who believes, as he himself observed in the *Life of Milton,* that "we are perpetually moralists," that the distinguishing condition of humanity is moral involvement. In the unending conflict of good and evil, happiness and pain, obligation and indolence that is the warfare of life the only neutrals are the brutes. One may pass or fail, but there is no cutting the exam except at the price of dehumanization. "To strive with difficulties, and to conquer them," he wrote,

> is the highest human felicity; the next, is to strive, and deserve to conquer: but he whose life has passed without a contest, and who can boast neither success nor merit, can survey himself only as a useless filler of existence; and if he is content with his own character, must owe his satisfaction to insensibility.

These words from the *Adventurer* can be matched by others of similar burden scattered throughout the prose works.

To many people any reference to this side of Johnson's character calls up an unlovely image of that old man in Boswell's *Life* so often heard to pass dogmatic judgment on the frailties of others. There were such outbursts of course, though they may owe more to irascibility than to settled moral intolerance. And although this image is more caricature than portrait it does raise the question of Johnson's sincerity. We know, in fact can learn from Johnson himself, that the commonest mask of the hypocrite is the constant advocacy of virtue. This was not true of him. As assurance that Samuel Johnson did not moralize in order to win social approval there is the warrant of his life. He was a pious man in an age not much given to piety; a Christian doubtful of no one's salvation

so much as his own, who refused to flatter the pride of
the rich and was apparently incapable of condemning
the sins of the poor. He detested every form of injustice,
and in a society that had managed by ingenious rational-
ization to assuage its conscience about Negro slavery
never ceased to excoriate it as the worst of evils. A man
of moderate means, he used the bulk of his income to
maintain a group of indigents in his house in London.
Johnson was in politics a Tory and in faith an Anglican,
and never disguised his disapproval of Whigs or Dis-
senters. Yet it "was not only in his book but in his mind
that orthodoxy was united with charity," as he himself
wrote of the hymnist Isaac Watts.

My reason for this brief digression into the life and
character of the man is that to a greater extent than with
any other famous critic Johnson's critical orientation can
be rightly apprehended only in such a context. His most
characteristic statements about writers and their craft are
referable not to any distinctively literary credo but to the
overriding Christian humanism of which many of the
norms expressed in his criticism were only a special extension. When the typical Augustan critic spoke of the
writer as a teacher or public benefactor it was in order
to emphasize his special role and to set him somewhat
above ordinary men in this particular respect. The terms
of his argument encouraged the public to think of the
poet's teaching as unique in kind and precious, and thus
to grant him a social function for which there was no
proper substitute. The tendency of Johnson's didacticism
is just the reverse. For him it is always a writer's duty to
leave the world better than he found it because that is
the duty of every man whatever his calling. The vicious
poet traduced his manhood more than his craft.

This is not to suggest that Johnson's moralism was
essentially at odds with the intellectual temper of his age.
Quite the opposite is true. One aspect of neoclassical
thought, a major strand of its Platonic inheritance, is
the idea that truth and goodness imply each other. In the

eighteenth-century intellectual's exaltation of human reason there was always the assumption, tacit if not expressed, that clear thinking could hardly end in corrupt principles. This assumption, which can be traced back to the "right Reason" of an earlier humanism, hardens in Johnson's thought into an axiom that is as much a part of his literary criticism as of any other branch of his thought. It is not of a philosopher nor in *Rasselas* or a *Rambler* paper, but of Shakespeare and in the *Preface* that he asserts his conviction that "he that thinks reasonably must think morally." Here, in capsule version, is an article of faith to which many humanists have subscribed, including some who have written literary criticism.

Nonetheless, it is a matter of simple candor to declare right off that when moral considerations intrude into Johnson's criticism the result is usually regrettable. Where we do not resent the intrusion is where instead of judging a work on purely moral grounds, he gives over literary criticism altogether and simply moralizes on a literary text. How much store Johnson put in poetic edification may be guessed from his note on Macbeth's retort to his wife in Act I, scene vii:

> *I dare do all that may become a man,*
> *Who dares do more is none.*

He thought these few words worthy "to bestow immortality on the author, though all his other productions had been lost," because they so effectively destroy the sophism of Lady Macbeth's appeal to courage as an inducement to murder: an old dodge that had sometimes "animated the house-breaker, and sometimes the conqueror. . . ." Few readers will complain when the somewhat extravagant critical evaluation is so amply compensated for by the moralist's exposure of yet another admirable evasion of whoremaster man and by the deft, almost Swiftian satire that deflates military grandeur to burglary.

Johnson's morally oriented readings are not always so rewarding. Sometimes they can be embarrassingly trite, as in the General Observation on *Timon of Athens*, where we are solemnly informed that this play is a powerful warning that "ostentatious liberality" wins flattery but not friendship. Often they are simply heavy-handed, as in the note on Act IV, scene iii of *Romeo and Juliet*, where Juliet gets rid of the Nurse by telling her she wants to be alone to pray. Remarking that this heroine "plays most of her pranks under the appearance of religion," Johnson speculates that in the play Shakespeare may have meant to punish Juliet's hypocrisy. On rare occasions Johnson goes beyond warping critical judgment to produce that momentary blackout of appreciation that led him to dismiss Pope's tender *Elegy to the Memory of an Unfortunate Lady* in a single damning sentence: "Poetry has not often been worse employed than in dignifying the amorous fury of a raving girl."

Perhaps the most offensive displays of Johnson's moralism are those that appear side-by-side with his finest critical passages, such as the inspired "anatomy" of "unimitated, unimitable Falstaff" in the Notes to 2 *Henry IV*, a single paragraph which does more to explain Sir John's paradoxical charm than Maurice Morgann's whole laborious *Essay on the Dramatic Character of Falstaff* (1777). The thief, glutton, coward, and boaster is relieved, Johnson writes, "by the most pleasing of all qualities, perpetual gaiety, by an unfailing power of exciting laughter. . . ." Falstaff commits no grave crime; "his licentiousness is not so offensive but that it may be borne for his mirth." The man who could write this was clearly a man delighted by Falstaff and a critic who knew how to express his experience in a way that conveys more than a hint of what makes him the greatest of comic figures. Yet, in a jarring shift of tone, Johnson must immediately append another paragraph spelling out a "moral to be drawn from this representation" scarcely in keeping with his analysis and even less so with the total import of the play. The gay, hardly offensive Falstaff suddenly becomes a dangerous and unsafe companion. One can only reflect how much more suited to our moral experience is the defense offered by pre-Collier comic theory: Falstaff combats vice by making it ridiculous.

The sentence pronounced against Pope's *Unfortunate Lady* is a glaring example of the kind of thing that has led some students of Johnson to complain that his moral yardstick is at odds with his demand for realism in literature. Any reader may be excused for asking why amorous girls and their ravings are not a part of that true state of sublunary nature which this critic so constantly praises writers for reflecting accurately. Nor is it satisfactory to reply that in this instance it is not the subject but Pope's sympathetic treatment of suicide that Johnson deplores. Waiving as irrelevant the poor light this throws on his own charity, one boggles at the implications for a good portion of the world's literature if a poet may not compassionate a sinner in verse.

It seems clear that Johnson was impelled to critical injustice of this kind by an exaggerated estimate of the moral and social effects of literature. Whether he may not for this very reason be now salutary in an age increasingly automatic in its opposition to any and all censorship of any and all books is not at the moment in question. In his view a literary work was, at best and worst, an exemplum. That an author had it in his power to harm society was only the other side to the coin of his primary obligation to improve it. At times Johnson seems almost fearful of books. His own hypersensitive imagination made him unusually susceptible to literary suggestion. We can guess how much the grave Rambler's scorn for romances owes to his having been addicted to them in early life. Throughout his criticism, but especially in his commentary on Shakespeare, there are scattered indications of how deeply his emotions were stirred by depictions of passion or violence. One note confesses his relief at having finished revising the murder scene in *Othello,* because, quite simply, "it is not to be endured." The audience in a theater, he had argued in the *Preface,* is at every moment fully conscious of the unreality of the persons and events it is watching. Johnson if anyone ought to have sensed how faulty this account of spectator psychology was, since so much of his own experience attested to the opposite extreme of reacting to the imaginary as though it were reality. The very language of Johnson's critical utterances reveals repeatedly how quickly aesthetic distance shrank to near zero whenever he confronted a piece of writing more than ordinarily emotive. Hamlet's expressed desire to send Claudius' soul to Hell he found "too horrible to be read or to be uttered." The words of his protest against the untimely death of Ophelia, "the young, the beautiful, the harmless, and the pious," are expressive of something close to real anguish.

It is in the light of this peculiar aspect of his personal psychology that we may best understand his adherence to poetic justice. The concatenation of epistemological assumptions that lay behind Thomas Rymer's original advocacy of this doctrine, which was outlined in Chapter II above, meant no more to Johnson than the similar rational considerations advanced by the early supporters of the unities of time and place. His rejection of these rules and his endorsement of poetic justice are based alike mainly on psychological grounds. Speaking of Thomas Otway's popular tragedy *The Orphan* in *The Lives of the Poets,* he concedes that its only appeal is to the affections. Still, he generalizes, "if the heart is interested" the lack of other qualities will never be missed. Like most critics—if one looks closely—Johnson tended to assume that others were bound to be affected by a given work as he was. No one's writings provide a better illustration than his that the prime critical virtue is not diffidence but rather that sincerity which, as Remy de Gourmont once wrote, consists in erecting one's personal impressions into laws. His confident statement in the *Life of Butler* that every reader is bored by the mythological materials in ancient poetry is only one among many others made in a serene assurance that his own strong distaste for mythology was universal. Johnson saw well enough that the law of poetic justice worked against the higher law of realistic representation. This much can be inferred from his willingness to excuse Addison's violation of poetic justice in *Cato*. Though some plays may "gratify our wishes," he observes, others ought to remind us of hard truths. But apart from the fear that readers may be tempted to wrongdoing by the spectacle of triumphant evil, his predominant opinion on the question was dictated by the heart's desire, by the reflection that everyone naturally loves to see innocence rewarded. This is his argument for preferring the happy ending Nahum Tate had supplied in his version of *King Lear*. So completely did his own love of justice suppress all other considerations, that the justice-loving Addison's preference for the original unhappy ending aroused no suspicion in Johnson's mind that the matter might not be quite so simple. And in the case of *Lear*, unfortunately, a sentimental generation of theatergoers had long ratified his personal taste.

Despite a strong emotional response to literature, however, and despite his appeal "from criticism to nature," from rational theory to the heart's desire, Johnson was no literary hedonist. According to his definition of poetry quoted earlier in this chapter, it is an art in which pleasure and the imagination subserve truth and reason. His concept of literary value is as rigorously utilitarian as any we encounter in the writings of the strictest neoclassics. In the Prologue which he wrote for David Garrick when the Drury Lane theater was opened in 1747, he was careful to speak of comedy and tragedy as supplying, respectively, "*useful* Mirth and *salutary* Woe." As Leavis suggests, he prefers an overt didacticism to the risk that a reader may miss the lesson. In the *Preface to Shake-*

speare he laments that this greatest of dramatists aimed more to please than to instruct, and the Notes to the plays abound in examples of what he meant. Typical of many others is one recording his indignation that Shakespeare expressed no disapproval, in 2 *Henry IV*, at John of Lancaster's base violation of his promise to exonerate the rebels. Yet if the quality of delighting, of captivating the reader's imagination, was not of itself sufficient to justify a work, Johnson leaves no doubt that it was a necessary cause of its value. Temperance and chastity, celebrated in Milton's *Comus,* stood high on Johnson's list of virtues; but in the *Life of Milton* he calls the masque "tediously instructive," because for various reasons he could get no pleasure from reading it. In its theory and practice Johnson's criticism everywhere gives added emphasis to the neoclassical faith that a good book was in some sense a moral book. But there is also his warning in the *Life of Dryden,* directed as much to poets in spite of Apollo as to purveyors of critical recipes, that "that book is good in vain which the reader throws away."

Just as Johnson's criterion of edification extends the classical doctrine of poetry's moral end, so his criterion of realism grows out of the classical demand for probability. What he did with it is equally regrettable. As he formulates it and as he applies it to particular works, he too frequently reduces the traditional neoclassical concept to a realism that comes perilously close to obliterating any distinction between a work of fiction and a factual report. Not always, of course. No one will quarrel with the norm of a conformity to nature by which he rates Otway's dramas above Dryden's, for example, nor with his occasional complaint, mild in any case, against the improbability of one of Shakespeare's plots. We can even relish the humorous sarcasm to which he is sometimes prompted by what he regards as a writer's foolish indulgence of fancy. In *Rambler* 37 it is turned against Spenser's attempt to reproduce the ungrammatical speech of rustics in his pastorals. "Surely," Johnson quips, "at the same time that a shepherd learns theology he may gain some acquaintance with his native language." And it must be a dull reader who cannot at once enjoy the fun and admit the critical pertinence of his finding it absurd in Dryden's *The Hind and the Panther* that "one beast should counsel another to rest her faith upon a pope and council." It may not be unfair to say that Dryden's allegory might have been contrived to resist the irony of Johnson's tough-minded contemplation. Nonetheless, the technique involves risks that he did not always avoid. In the *Life of Gray* it degenerates into a peevish literalism when he looks at the *Ode on a Distant Prospect of Eton College* and thinks the poet childish for asking Father Thames to tell him who now rolls the hoop and tosses the ball. It is difficult to see what there is in Gray's use of so innocent a convention as the apostrophe to merit Johnson's grumpy protest that "Father Thames has no better means of knowing than himself."

The fact is that Johnson's realism is vitiated by an intolerance of the fictive that is often critically debilitating. In his praise of Shakespeare's dialogue for being so lifelike that it can hardly claim "the merit of fiction" there is a certain unconscious irony, since in his mind fiction seems to have been only dubiously meritorious. The word fiction's pejorative connotation, of something not true, seems almost to have hypnotized his consciousness against any but a jaundiced admission of its innocent sense of an imaginative creation. The kind of writing he most favored was not novels or plays but, as he says in *Rambler* 60 among other places, biography; no other species is more useful or delightful. Because it relates the real doings of real men, biography is for Johnson at the top of a scale of literary value; at the bottom lies mythology, which he detested. With varying degrees of appropriateness he applies this scale to all sorts of literary composition. In *Adventurer* 92, devoted to a quite detailed analysis of Virgil's pastoral verse, he downgrades the much admired fifth *Eclogue* because it is so heavily mythological. His commendation goes instead to numbers one and ten because they celebrate "events that really happened"; in their superiority he sees proof that "the most artful fiction must give way to truth." Six years later, in *Idler* 89, we find him once again exalting biography above all other narrative forms and coupling the imagined characters and action of fictional writing with the "useless" truth of the historian, things of no practical value to ordinary men and women.

All of which leads naturally to the notorious treatment of *Lycidas* in the *Life of Milton*, a misjudgment that Johnson would now presumably have to retract, inasmuch as the poem has since passed his own final test of literary merit, "continuance of esteem." In judging some of his strictures on this beautiful elegy, those aimed at its alleged harsh diction, imperfect rhymes, and unpleasant versification, we ought charitably to allow for the gap between its form and style and Johnson's Augustan taste. But to dismiss his whole argument against it, with Professor Bate, as just another of the great critic's "few quaint misfires" [7] is to overlook the weighty evidence of parallel arguments scattered throughout his criticism. This evidence shows Johnson's poor opinion of *Lycidas* to have been instead the most lamentable result of his radical antipathy to the fictive. One symptom of this antipathy is his frequently expressed dislike of pastoral. Because the pastoral poet treated persons and situations either totally idealized or known to very few, he taught nothing a reader could apply to life; and, as the critic predictably remarks, *Lycidas* is in pastoral form, "easy, vulgar, and therefore disgusting."

But this is not all. The poem further offends by being a bad elegy because it is false and insincere. Johnson bases this conclusion on two kinds of evidence that exemplify the most crippling aspects of his realism. One is external and biographical: we know Milton and Edward King were never shepherds. The other is internal and psychological: the poem is filled with conventional allusions to berries, myrtle, ivy, satyrs, and fauns. "Where there is leisure for fiction there is little grief." This line of reasoning is fundamental in Johnson's literary evaluation. In the first of the *Lives of the Poets* he turns it against Cowley's love poems. Cowley, we recall, had confessed to singing only an imaginary love, like many another literary amorist; but for Johnson that was enough to condemn his poems, because "he that professes love ought to feel its power." Without an apparent sincerity the poet fails to convince a reader that he really grieves or loves, an objection that supposes a poem to be a mere instrument for communicating emotion or perhaps only information about emotion. The love elegies of James Hammond receive the same censure. Of one of Hammond's highly fanciful stanzas Johnson thinks it relevant to ask whether the "nymph" addressed could be blamed for rejecting "a swain of so little meaning." No doubt the question is posed less in sober earnest than as a way of satirizing Hammond's obscurity; nonetheless, its point depends upon an instrumentalism seriously entertained.

No fair assessment of Johnson's critical achievement can overlook the confusion of art and life implied in so unsophisticated a version of expressionism; one rejected, it should be noted, by the neoclassical Dryden as well as by the romantic Coleridge, and widely discredited in twentieth-century poetic theory, including the criticism of Johnson's advocate T. S. Eliot. It is not a momentary aberration of thought into which he is betrayed by one or another poem or poet he dislikes, but a constant motif in his critical writing, explicitly formulated again in the brief *Life of Hammond*: "Where there is fiction, there is no passion." The elegist must really mourn, the sonneteer truly be in love. Some of Johnson's favorite poetry might have taught him better. A modern reader may attain a certain imaginative reconstruction of the taste that could not relish Milton's great elegy by turning to one by Thomas Tickell *On the Death of Mr. Addison*

(1721), of which Johnson wrote in the *Lives* that there was no "more sublime or more elegant funeral-poem to be found in the whole compass of English literature." There is nothing surprising in this encomium; Tickell's poem is a good one, and in a typically Augustan mode as remote from *Lycidas* as is possible in a poem of the same genre. One wonders, though, that so candid a critic should have passed in silence over some lines near the beginning which directly challenge his own assurance that feigned emotion cannot make good poetry. Tickell wrote:

> Slow comes the verse, that real woe inspires:
> Grief unaffected suits but ill with art,
> Or flowing numbers with a bleeding heart.

Here and there, it is true, Johnson seems to allow exceptions to his severe principle, one of them applied generally to epitaphs, in writing which, Boswell quotes him as saying, "a man is not upon oath." This particular relaxation of truth seems less an aesthetic license, however, than an indulgence to the dead extended equally to Dryden's "insincere" praise of Anne Killigrew's creative talents in what Johnson considered the noblest ode in the English language. More promising, had he conformed to its implications elsewhere, is his defense of Shakespeare's hyperbole in *Romeo and Juliet* of a beautiful woman outshining the stars. Comparing it to Pope's image in the *Rape of the Lock,*

> Sol through white curtains shot a tim'rous ray
> And ope'd those eyes that must eclipse the day,

he observes that in both poets something that is "philosophic nonsense" makes "poetical sense." Similarly, the persuasion that fiction must always give way to truth did not spoil Johnson's appreciation of fictitious Shakespearean creations like Caliban nor get in the way of his delight in that "race of aerial people, never heard of before," the sylphs of Pope's *Rape*. But this freedom of the imagination from the demands of truth and probability Johnson was unwilling to extend to lyric and didactic verse, where the poet is presumed to be speaking in his own person. Nothing is more foreign to his critical thought than an allowance for the lyrical "as if," the poetic mask. He knew the pretense, observing in the *Life of Pope* that poets do not always write what they think or feel. But he could not countenance it, and so takes exception to Pope's expressing an indifference to wealth, fame, and success in his moral poems which he did not always evince in his life.

Perhaps nothing Johnson wrote about the poet's imitation of reality is better known than the assertion in the *Preface to Shakespeare* that only general representations can give lasting pleasure, and Imlac's instruction to the Prince, in *Rasselas,* that the poet's business is to capture nature's "general properties," not to number the streaks of the tulip. Here again Johnson was only endorsing an idea widely held since the Restoration. His friend Reynolds preached the same doctrine. Minute discriminations of the particular, he taught in the third *Discourse,* are a proper concern of flower painters and shell collectors. Like the philosopher, the artist will instead "represent in every one of his figures the character of its species." At the same time that Reynolds and Johnson were affirming the aesthetic of generality, however, it was being denied by admirers of the picturesque and the unusual. The theoretical disagreement, interestingly, did not always enforce a disagreement in taste. Johnson and Joseph Warton both admired Homer, Johnson because he dealt in the general, Warton because his images, like those of Shakespeare, were of particulars. Among modern poems, both listed Thomson's *Seasons* as a favorite: Warton because of such delicious details as the single falling leaf and the white shower of thistledown, cited in the *Essay on Pope,* Johnson because Thomson's attention to the minute did not prevent his comprehension of vast general effects.

In another sense though, the psychology of Johnson's personal taste played its usual part in his attitude toward this question. For Reynolds the theory of generality had a sufficient basis in the reigning conception of nature. Since no two blades of grass are exactly alike, as he noted in *Idler* 82, the painter selects for his model the most beautiful, which is necessarily the most general. Though Johnson clearly enough subscribed to this familiar conception, it was only after it had passed the test to which he characteristically subjected all critical reasons, that of his own taste and experience. Especially revealing in this regard are the contrasting verdicts he and Warton pronounced on Pope's extended comparison, in the *Essay on Criticism*, of an aspiring poet to an alpine traveler dismayed to find that "Hills peep o'er hills and alps on alps arise." In the *Life of Pope* Johnson judged this to be perhaps the finest simile in English poetry. But in his own study of Pope's art Warton complained that the images in the comparison were too general and indistinct to be effective.

That Johnson had a real fondness for the abstract word and the generalized conception can be inferred not only from the things he singled out for praise or censure but also from the poetry he himself wrote:

> Let observation with extensive view,
> Survey mankind from China to Peru.

In these opening lines of *The Vanity of Human Wishes* Coleridge (as reported by J. P. Collier) could find nothing but "mere bombast and tautology; as much as to say, 'Let observation with extensive observation observe mankind extensively.'" Yet it may not be entirely perverse to suggest that what Coleridge regarded (fairly enough by his lights) as a tasteless and pompous redundancy can strike a less prejudiced ear as attractive for a reverberative grandeur of language and conception that has its own special if limited beauty. At least it seems to have been so for Johnson. There is reason for thinking that in him the century's predilection for the general was especially intense. Since general conceptions and the abstractions by which they are verbalized are by their very nature departures from the real, their fascination for Johnson may seem at odds with the temperamental realism of the man who confuted Berkeley by kicking a stone. But the very intensity of his predilection consists in the fact that he felt a generality to be more nearly real than ideal. Professor William Wimsatt has pointed out that

> if he is interested in generality, in the classes to which things belong, the aspects which unify groups of objects, he becomes at moments even more interested in these aspects as things in themselves, as metaphysical realities.[8]

It is easy to imagine that a mind so constituted should have responded with almost sensuous immediacy to abstractions in a poem.

When Boswell said it was strange that the *Journey to the Western Islands* had not sold well, Johnson replied, "Yes sir; for in that book I have told the world a great deal that they did not know before." Novelty, here thought sufficient to recommend a travel book, is a quality he also valued in poetry and evoked as often as he did the ideal of generality. To expect even imaginative literature to provide information consists well enough with the utilitarian-didactic view of its function so central to Johnson's thinking. Yet more obviously than with other aspects of his theory he justifies this one less on *a priori* moral and intellectual principles than on grounds of psychological necessity. A ready prey to boredom himself, like Pascal Johnson saw in imaginative restlessness a fundamental condition of humanity, needing constant appeasement.

In some discussions of Johnson's literary thought, however, the ideal of originality has received distorted emphasis. However central to his psychological theory, in his criticism it is subjected to the limitations imposed by the higher requirements of generality and universal appeal. Fanciful invention, he observes in the *Preface to Shakespeare,* can for a while satisfy "that novelty of which the common satiety of life sends us all in quest," but lasting pleasure comes only from "just representations of general nature." Undeniably there are many places in *The Lives of the Poets* where, in apparent disregard of his own principle, Johnson exalts mere originality above every other consideration. Among these is his perverse complaint that the truths of *Paradise Lost* failed to surprise because they were known in advance. This is part of his disapproval of all religious verse: pious sentiments cannot be new. Though Isaac Watts was included in the collection of English poets at Johnson's own suggestion, he nonetheless finds Watts' hymns unsatisfactory because his subject binds him to constant repetition. To James Thomson, on the other hand, he accords "praise of the highest kind" for his originality.

If these opinions seem hardly consonant with a demand for generality, it should nevertheless be noted that what Johnson appreciates in Thomson is the freshness of his manner of thought and his expression. The inherent disadvantage under which the devotional poet labored consisted precisely in being denied these adornments since, as Johnson remarks elsewhere in the *Lives,* religion, a higher thing than poetry, can "receive no grace from novelty of sentiment, and very little from novelty of expression." Certainly he had no use for the kind of originality that is attained by dreaming up notions or devising images which the writer is sure no one else would ever hit on. Of this quality Johnson thought the metaphysical poets of the previous century had more than enough, and when he wrote the *Life of Cowley* made his contempt for it unmistakably plain in his comment on a stanza of John Donne's *Obsequies to the Lord Harrington:* "Who but Donne," he asks, "would have thought that a good man is a telescope?" Johnson's originality is reconcilable with universal appeal, the originality for which he commends four stanzas of the *Elegy in a Country Churchyard* in the *Life of Gray*. These stanzas contain notions he has never seen elsewhere yet is convinced he has always felt. Johnson cavilled at Pope's celebrated definition of wit. Nonetheless, when he lauds the *Elegy* for its many "images which find a mirror in every mind" and for "sentiments to which every bosom returns an echo," he implies a criterion of poetic excellence remarkably similar to the

> *Something whose truth convinced at sight we find,*
> *That gives us back the image of our mind.*

Both critics envisage a mutual accommodation of the novel and the universal that is ideal and unmistakably neoclassical.

THE CRITICAL PRACTICE

My excuse for what some readers may feel to be a violent and arbitrary separation of Johnson's general views of literature and his applied criticism must be the conviction that in Johnson the critic who endures is the practical critic, and never more than when his specific analyses and judgments overcome or by-pass the several principles examined in the last section. I largely subscribe to the opinion of Allen Tate that Johnson's "theories (if his ideas ever reach the level of theoretical abstraction) are perhaps too simple for our taste and too improvised; but his reading is disciplined and acute." [9]

Because Johnson's critical greatness lies mainly in his acute readings, it is best conveyed by what may be called an anthological method, in which illustrative quotation takes the place of analysis. Yet one returns often to Johnson's critical works for more than accurate interpretations. In them as in all he wrote there is the accent of a remarkable personality; and there is the unique style and the sometimes surprising vocabulary, reminding us that before he wrote the *Preface* and the *Lives* he was

famous for a dictionary. By contrast with Dryden's con-
versational ease and Addison's graceful elegance, Johnson's
prose is formal and ceremonious, sometimes even ponder-
ous and too noticeably labored. He prefers the learned
word of Latin derivation to its synonym in commoner
use. A large proportion of his sentences is made up of
clauses and phrases antithetically balanced; and he falls
readily into alliteration ("predict the progress of the
passions"). These qualities, more marked in the earlier
work than in the later, can in large doses become tiresome, as anyone may discover by reading through several
Rambler essays at a sitting. But if his vocabulary is often
startlingly recondite (*evulsion, extrusion, subduct, re-
frigerate*), at their best and most characteristic Johnson's
Latinate abstractions are made to express precise shades
of meaning. Thus he writes that Dryden could imagine
love only when it was mixed with some other passion:
"when it was *inflamed* by rivalry, or *obstructed* by difficulties; when it *invigorated* ambition, or *exasperated*
revenge." In *The Lives of the Poets* this manner is varied
by plainer language and often enlivened by touches of
humor like the reference to an English *Aeneid* of one
Dr. Brady, "which when dragged into the world did not
live long enough to cry."

Virtually all Johnson's literary criticism can be found
in his periodical writing, the *Rambler, Idler,* and *Adven-
ture* papers, in occasional prefaces, in his edition of
Shakespeare's plays, and in *The Lives of the Poets*. The
latter two will show us Johnson at his critical best. The
well-known *Preface* that introduces the Shakespeare has
so often been judged out of its historical context that I
have thought it best to postpone it to the next chapter.
Although the notes to the text of the plays are mainly of
concern to specialists in Shakespeare or in Johnson, some
of them are interesting to the ordinary reader for what
they reveal of their author's personal temperament and
taste. Often believed to be dogmatic and opinionated,
Johnson appears quite otherwise in these annotations.

Explaining textual obscurities, he sometimes offers his own emendation, sometimes endorses one by a previous editor, Theobald or Hanmer or Warburton. Always more determined to restore Shakespeare than to display his own ingenuity, he is quick to register caution and to confess his own uncertainties. He observes of a passage in *As You Like It* that "elegance alone will not justify alteration." He thinks his own interpretation of a difficult place in *All's Well* "more acute and more refined" than Warburton's, but will let the reader judge. He would like to follow that editor in rejecting another passage of this play as spurious, "for a commentator naturally wishes to reject what he cannot understand." But, he concludes, "I know not what to do with the passage"—a display of editorial humility as disarming as it is rare.

As we should expect, many notes exemplify Johnson's literary biases or those of his age, sometimes amusingly. There is the attitude toward language decorum for instance. The line in *Richard II*, "Which serves as paste and cover to our bones," he finds to be a "metaphor not of the most sublime kind, taken from a *pie*." And of course there are the despised puns, deplored as "fatal Cleopatras" in the *Preface*, here called Shakespeare's "darling equivocations." To eighteenth-century readers Shakespeare's habit of playing on words even in the most awesome situations was simply unaccountable. That he should indulge it in Lady Macbeth at the moment of the murder strains Johnson's belief: "Could Shakespeare possibly mean to play upon the similitude of *gild* and *guilt* [?]" Other annotations will puzzle a modern reader who forgets the high value Augustans placed on perspicuity. Richard II's remark to the Queen, "I am sworn brother, sweet, to grim Necessity," clear enough to us, Johnson feels it necessary to elucidate by paraphrase. Precise expression, he notes elsewhere, was not Shakespeare's strong point. But since most neoclassical criticism renders a largely negative verdict on Shakespeare's language, feeling it to be harsh, obscure, bombastic, it is instructive to learn from these *Notes* that Johnson was not entirely deaf to the verbal music. A line spoken by the Archbishop in the first act of *Henry V*, "The air, a charter'd libertine, is still," strikes him as "exquisitely beautiful."

It was not the free-ranging imagery and blank verse of the Elizabethans, however, but the restricted idiom and decorously modeled couplets of the eighteenth-century poets to which Johnson's ear was most happily attuned. Chiefly for this reason *The Lives of the Poets* is his critical masterpiece and most flawlessly when he writes on Dryden and Pope. Strictly speaking, Johnson's taste was atavistic. To the various departures from the Augustan ideal espoused by such contemporaries as the Warton brothers, Hurd, Percy, Macpherson, Gray, Collins, and Akenside he was almost entirely unsympathetic. Although he speaks highly of the first volume of Joseph Warton's *Essay on Pope,* nothing was more repugnant to Johnson's own ideas of literary excellence than that critic's admiration of Gray's bardic poems, to say nothing of his unfortunate enthusiasm for the Gothic excesses of *The Castle of Otranto.* His conclusion that Pope's poems were not "of the most poetic species" typified the critical revisionism that was challenged by Johnson's rhetorical question: "If Pope be not a poet, where is poetry to be found?"

Johnson's favorite among the *Lives* was that on Cowley, of most interest to our century for its analysis of metaphysical poetry. Even modern enthusiasts of John Donne have admitted the accuracy of Johnson's description of how the wit of the metaphysicals manifests itself "as a kind of *discordia concors,* a combination of dissimilar images, or discovery of occult resemblances in things apparently unlike." But though he acknowledges the intellectual quality of their verse he questions their right to be called poets, since he cannot see that they imitated either nature or life. Twentieth-century commentators, ascribing this judgment to a misapplication of narrow neoclassical standards, have severely criticized Johnson's low estimate of Donne's poetry. In rebuttal W. R. Keast argued plausibly that Johnson's evaluation may not be so far from the mark as Donne's advocates charge, since few of his poems come near the excellence of *A Valediction: Forbidding Mourning*.[10] This argument would be a better defense of Johnson's critical discernment if he had not quoted sixteen lines of that very poem without the slightest commendation of it, and if he had not—unkindest cut of all—expressed his uncertainty whether the celebrated simile of the twin compasses was more ingenious than absurd.

The *Life of Milton* is a mixed performance, especially on the minor poems. Johnson was once heard to say that like Phidias, Milton "could cut a Colossus out of a rock, but could not cut heads out of cherry stones." He does admire *L'Allegro* and *Il Penseroso*, calling them "two noble efforts of imagination," but passes over the sonnets as not worth critical examination, influenced perhaps by his belief that this Italian verse form was not suited to the English language. *Comus* fares better under his inspection than *Lycidas;* he finds it "truly poetical," deficient as drama, and rather tiresome to read. On *Samson Agonistes* Johnson had always been a dissenter, convinced that only learned bigotry, prepossessed in its favor because of its Greek tragic form, had given the drama its reputation. He thinks it ill-constructed, its beginning and end causally related by no middle. In most of these appraisals one or another of Johnson's personal biases can be detected.

By contrast, the pages devoted to *Paradise Lost* are a model of critical objectivity. Johnson conceals neither his disapproval of Milton's personal character, politics, and religious views, nor his distaste for the blank verse and the "Babylonish dialect" of Milton's epic. Yet the praise he gives it is discerning and generous. Its moral purpose he thinks admirable. Its structure, comprising the Aristotelian beginning, middle, and end, is perfect, every part necessary to the design. The demonic characters are judiciously discriminated, with exact consistency, and the human pair endowed with appropriate manners and feelings. Like Dennis and others before him, Johnson sees sublimity as the predominant quality of *Paradise Lost,* "sublimity variously modified, sometimes descriptive, sometimes argumentative."

There are of course faults—"for faults and defects every work of man must have." Predictably, Johnson regrets that the central truths of the poem are "too important to be new." Like most other readers at the time he feels the allegory of Sin and Death to be a blemish, and like many readers today he sees the inherent impossibility of describing the "agency of spirits" and the resulting incongruousness of the war in heaven. None of this prevents him from concluding, however, that anyone who thinks the defects of "that wonderful performance" are not far outweighed by its beauties should be "pitied for want of sensibility." It is, he says, an impartial critic's duty to point out the shortcomings of Milton as of lesser men; "but such is the power of his poetry, that his call is obeyed without resistance, the reader feels himself in captivity to a higher and nobler mind, and criticism sinks in admiration."

Despite the excellence of this critique, it is surpassed by those in the *Lives* of Dryden and Pope, because when he turned to the Augustan masters Johnson's "criticism" and admiration were more often at one. True enough, one can find in these two *Lives* opinions and attitudes from which to dissent. Few people who enjoy reading Dryden's first *Ode for Saint Cecilia's Day* will share Johnson's objection to the word *diapason* or admit the general ban on the use of technical words in poetry on which it is based. Johnson thought it a major objection against the *Essay on Man* that it can be reduced in paraphrase to a series of trite metaphysical and moral maxims; we do not think so. But the few statements in these *Lives* annulled by time and altered taste are outshone by several passages that hold their rank among the finest ever written on these two poets. Probably no one has ever characterized Dryden's literary criticism more unerringly or more eloquently than Johnson when he contrasts it to that of Rymer.

> With Dryden we are wandering in quest of truth; whom we find, if we find her at all, dressed in the graces of elegance; and, if we miss her, the labour of the pursuit rewards itself; we are led only through fragrance and flowers. Rymer, without taking a nearer, takes a rougher way; every step is to be made through thorns and brambles; and Truth, if we meet her, appears repulsive by her mien, and ungraceful by her habit. Dryden's criticism has the majesty of a queen; Rymer's has the ferocity of a tyrant.

This gem of comparative evaluation is equaled, or almost so, by descriptions of Dryden's style in prose and verse. In subtlety of discrimination it is perhaps surpassed by another in the *Life of Pope*:

> Of genius, that power which constitutes a poet; that quality without which judgment is cold, and knowledge is inert; that energy which collects, combines, amplifies, and animates; the superiority must, with some hesitation, be allowed to Dryden. It is not to be inferred that of this poetical vigour Pope had only a little, because Dryden had more; for every other writer since Milton must give place to Pope; and even of Dryden it must be said, that, if he has brighter paragraphs, he has not better poems. Dryden's performances were always hasty, either excited by some external occasion, or extorted by domestic necessity; he composed without consideration, and published without correction. What his mind could supply at call, or gather in one excursion, was all that he sought, and all that he gave. The dilatory caution of Pope enabled him to condense his sentiments, to multiply his images, and to accumulate all that study might produce or chance might supply. If the flights of Dryden therefore are higher, Pope continues longer on the wing. If of Dryden's fire the blaze is brighter, of Pope's the

heat is more regular and constant. Dryden often sur-
passes expectation, and Pope never falls below it. Dryden is read with frequent astonishment, and Pope with
perpetual delight.

Except that no brief sketch of a great poet's manner can
ever quite satisfy the conception of his more ardent
admirers, Johnson's hope that his comparison would be
found just, "when it is well considered," is entirely reasonable.

Though he confesses some partiality for Dryden, in
many ways it is Pope who represents Johnson's poetic
ideal. In him alone he found, "in proportions very nicely
adapted to each other," invention, imagination, and judgment, all the qualities required for genius. In his discussion of Pope's poems the excessive preoccupation with
novelty and truth that so often blurs Johnson's aesthetic
vision elsewhere is least obtrusive, their claims over-
borne by an unreflecting delight in the poet's art. The
section of the *Essay on Criticism* showing how the
sound of a verse should echo the sense offended his
settled conviction that the notion of representative meter
was illusory. Yet he finds that youthful creation adorned
and dignified by every mode of excellence that belongs to
didactic writing. *The Rape of the Lock* is not perfect:
the sylphs have no effective part in the action; the game
of ombre is useless; worst of all, the poem is morally
flimsy. "But what are such faults to so much excellence?"
If in the *Essay on Man* Pope fails lamentably in his
ambitious aim to instruct his readers, it is still true that
in many places the brilliant adornments, the sweet
melody, the varied dignity and delicacy of the lines "en-
chain philosophy, suspend criticism, and oppress judgment by overpowering pleasure." And so it goes. Johnson's
frequent references to the suspension or "sinking" of
criticism in the presence of great art is a kind of unconscious confession of the irrelevance of his own criteria
to the literature he loved best. To this literature he could

pay the full tribute of appreciative recognition only by holding the criteria in abeyance.

The *Life of Addison* ranks nearly with those of Milton, Dryden, and Pope. The *Lives* of Rochester, Congreve, Gay, Thomson, Gray, and perhaps one or two others retain interest. Some, mostly those on poets no longer read, are nugatory. The one on Richard Savage, written much earlier, is admirable as biography. Most disappointing for its grudging appraisal and its brevity is the *Life of Swift,* in which Johnson's critical powers apparently failed to repeat the triumph over his moral disapproval attained in the *Life of Milton*.

Yet a case can be made for reading the *Lives* in their entirety. Taken together, they exhibit every facet of Johnson's critical thought, the full gamut of his limitations and his virtues. They remain, the best of them, models of biographical criticism and—what with their author would count for much—they are never dull. Most important, they contain more examples of descriptive evaluation like those quoted above than can be found in all the rest of his critical writings. And it is on these, the products of an analytical skill turned on poem or poet, that Johnson's claim to critical eminence chiefly rests.

VI *THE NEOCLASSICAL SHAKESPEARE*

Shakespeare, Alexander Pope observed in the Preface to his edition of the plays, is "the fairest and fullest subject for criticism" because every kind of beauty and every kind of blemish can be found in his works. To judge from the extent and the quality of the Shakespearian criticism of that period, most other neoclassical critics agreed. Broadly speaking, there is truth in the common supposition that between the Restoration and the close of the eighteenth century Shakespeare's reputation rose from the nadir of Rymer's wholesale condemnation to a chorus of praise fulsome enough to have been called idolatrous. Yet at no time during these years can it be said that Shakespeare was neglected or generally disliked by his countrymen. Rymer's attacks, one should remember, were prompted in the first place by the continued popularity of the plays, along with some by Beaumont and Fletcher, on the London stage.

The Augustans' attitude toward Shakespeare was actually twofold, or threefold. As readers, indeed as English readers, they were enchanted by many things in his works, puzzled and repelled by others. As spokesmen of a new classicism they had on the whole to disapprove of him, and that in proportion to the degree of their enthusiasm for the French critical norms. Their total reaction was complex, not simply a matter of conflict between heart and head. The heart itself was divided because the new critical canons were accompanied, either as cause or result, by an altered poetic palate to which Shakespeare seems to have tasted bittersweet. The greatest writer of the age, Dryden, typifies the general attitude in his several capacities: The playwright deplored Shakespeare's careless plotting and took him as model for his best tragedy; the critic disapproved his violation of the unities and praised him above all other dramatists; the reader complained of his bombastic style and called him divine. In short, Dryden pronounced this greatest of the giants before the flood "the very Janus of poets," who wore "almost everywhere two faces; and you have scarce begun to admire the one, ere you despise the other."

Admired he was nonetheless, sometimes against critical conscience, and familiar enough to the fastidious patrons of the Restoration theater for Dryden to be sure they would recognize

> *Fall on, Macduff*
> *And Cursed be he that first cries Hold, enough,*

when quoted by Palamede in *Marriage a-la-mode* (1673). Though the critics laughed at him, according to Edward Phillips in *Theatrum Poetarum* (1675), Shakespeare was a better poet than many more learned and refined. Those who voiced the common objection to his rude unpolished style also attested to his power over the passions of his audience and to the naturalness of his characters. Sir William Temple spoke of people shedding tears at some of the tragedies. The Earl of Mulgrave in 1682 anticipated Dr. Johnson in calling Falstaff unimitable; so did Shaftesbury when he approved of the total absence in *Hamlet* of the "blustering heroism" found in modern tragedy. Sketching out a rejoinder to Rymer's rationalist strictures, Dryden quoted René Rapin to the effect that the beauty of a tragedy lay not in its plot but in natural and passionate speech; then he added the curt notation: "So are Shakespeare's."

As suggested in an earlier chapter, it is instructive to notice what was liked or disliked. In this regard what is often most revealing is the neoclassic critics' silence on features of a given play which later commentary has taught us to admire. Surely we are told something about the eighteenth-century poetic ideal—though it were a nice question to say precisely what—from the very fact that Pope and Johnson take no notice whatever of certain soliloquies, for example, which every school child was once forced to memorize and which are now enshrined in phonographic recordings. The comparison which Dryden drew in the Preface to *Troilus and Cressida* (1679) between the patriotic veneration Englishmen felt for Shakespeare and that accorded Aeschylus by the Athenians validates T. S. Eliot's statement that in every period, the neoclassical included, Shakespeare has been highly respected.[1] The danger lies in assuming the ground of that respect to be always the same or approximately the same. It isn't; the Shakespeare of the age of Dryden and Pope is only partly the Shakespeare of the age of Eliot. Some of what no one for a long time has hesitated to include among the most remarkable soliloquies appear in *King Richard II*, those spoken by the King himself. There is also the famous encomium on England uttered by John of Gaunt in Act II. But if these passages impressed Dryden he gives no hint of it. What he chooses for special commendation in that play is rather the description of Richard being led in triumph through the London streets, because, as he explains, here is passion devoid of bombast. Most disturbing to readers of Shakespeare today, the bombast, rant, and fustian Dryden and his contemporaries so often complained of were apparently most in evidence in the great tirades pronounced by Lear, Hamlet, Macbeth, and Othello.

Dr. Johnson's opinion, expressed in the *Preface,* that Shakespeare was better at comedy than at tragedy is hard to reconcile with the very different estimate that has prevailed since Coleridge's day, and there is little point in trying to do so. At least Johnson knew that a Shakespeare tragedy was one thing and Addison's *Cato* another and quite different thing. This fact is worth remembering when we read in the anonymous *Remarks on the Tragedy of Hamlet Prince of Denmark* (1736) that "no tragic writer ever came up to Shakespeare, Rowe, and Mr. Addison." Pretty damning praise we think, though perhaps understandable from a critic (it may have been Thomas Hanmer) whose main generalization about Shakespeare's tragic masterpieces is that they are all impaired, *Hamlet* less than the others, by obscurity and bombast. For the historian of Shakespeare's reputation these opinions have one kind of interest; for the student of neoclassical criticism they have another, consisting principally in what they can tell him about what tragedy meant to eighteenth-century readers. That is, he might conceivably get a hint of it by discovering some quality common to *Cato* and the tragedies of Nicholas Rowe and Shakespeare, a quality likely to be located outside the twentieth-century appreciative focus. This kind of speculative enterprise is justified, however, only when a critic's opinion is corroborated by his contemporaries and so above suspicion of being merely a personal quirk. We know Pope disliked Macbeth's "Sleep that knits up the ravell'd sleeve of care," from which we might infer something about neoclassical blindness to Shakespeare's lyrical qualities—if we did not also know that both Pope and Rowe admired Viola's beautiful veiled confession of love in *Twelfth Night*.[2]

One of the many commonplaces to be found in Oliver Goldsmith's *Enquiry into the Present State of Polite Learning in Europe* is the wish that for England's honor and his own many of the scenes in Shakespeare's plays might be forgotten. In fact for a time some were. Playwrights and others whom we should now call producers felt it their duty to separate Shakespeare's gold from his dross by "pruning luxuriousness, correcting irregularity, rationalizing bombast, and elucidating obscurity," in the Johnsonesque phrases Francis Gentleman applied to Nahum Tate's emended version of *King Lear*. Gentleman also tells us that when David Garrick played *Macbeth* both the porter scene and the onstage slaughter of Macduff's wife and children were "commendably omitted in representation." Even the most ardent Shakespearians felt the intrusion of such farcical and violent materials to be a breach of tragic decorum. Joseph Warton, whose emancipation from Augustan norms went to the lengths of praising Dante and rating *King Lear* above Racine's *Athalie,* nevertheless could not stomach Shakespeare's fools. He thought them contrary to the nature of tragedy. He had the same objection to the gravediggers in *Hamlet,* whom even Dr. Johnson found just barely commendable.

Neoclassical didacticism was on the whole kinder to Shakespeare than neoclassical decorum. As we have seen, some critics, including Johnson, were disturbed by his indifference to poetic justice. Others, however, found him instructive enough. Shaftesbury praised him as much for "the justness of his moral" as for the lifelike quality of his persons; Lewis Theobald was pleased to discover in the plot of *Lear* useful cautions against rash bounty and filial ingratitude; and Johnson declared that "a system of civil and economical prudence" might be derived from Shakespeare's works. Rymer, as usual, provides the most extreme example of dissent. Desdemona's fate, he argued in the *Short View of Tragedy,* can only make the audience impugn divine justice. How much better, he suggested, if Othello had discovered the missing handkerchief rumpled in the wedding sheets. Then, seeing his wife lying in a trance of fright and apparently dead, he might in remorse have cut his throat, "by the good leave, and with the applause of all the Spectators. Who might thereupon have gone home with a quiet mind, admiring the beauty of Providence fairly and truly represented on the theatre." Rymer makes us smile, as no doubt he intended to do, ridicule being the readiest weapon in his critical arsenal. But his point is serious enough; the itch to "improve" Shakespeare was not his alone in Augustan times.

By defenders and detractors alike, Shakespeare, the natural poet, was set over against Ben Jonson, the poet of art. This view was given currency by Dryden though not initiated by him. If you compare these two Elizabethans, Richard Flecknoe wrote in 1664, "you shall see the difference betwixt Nature and Art . . . ." Earlier still, John Milton's *L'Allegro* had sung of "Jonson's learned sock" in contrast to Shakespeare's "native wood-notes wild." The usual tack was to ascribe the great dramatist's psychological depth and emotive power to a native gift while blaming his stylistic excesses and lapses of decorum on his supposed ignorance of the poet's craft. The dichotomy was not simple, however, not only because of the many semantic overtones of "nature" but even more because of the ambivalence of "art." Art often designated the rules, which in turn were means to the right imitation of nature, so that art and nature became in effect synonymous or at least interinvolved. The term art was also used to mean conscious craftsmanship, classical correctness, in contexts where nature meant the operation of untutored genius. The latter usage came into neoclassical terminology ultimately from Horace, who raised the question whether *Natura fieret laudabile carmen an arte,* that is, whether good poetry resulted from innate talent or acquired skill. His answer was both. In this opinion neoclassical critics generally followed him, though with an increasing emphasis on *natura* that contributed to the gradual enhancement of Shakespeare's reputation. In his edition of the *Epistula ad Pisones* Richard Hurd's note on this line reviews the controversy over which of the two qualities deserved precedence. "There was a time," he recalls,

> when the art of [Jonson] was set above the divine rap-
> tures of Shakespeare. The present age is well convinced
> of the mistake. And now the genius of Shakespeare is
> idolized in its turn. Happily for the public taste, it can
> scarcely be too much so.

This bit of Shakespeare idolatry, if it is fair to call it that,
dates from as early as 1753.

A more dominant critical strategy for reconciling a
taste for the great rough-hewn genius of Queen Elizabeth's time with a commitment to the literary aesthetic
of Queen Anne's was one first adopted by early eighteenth-century Spenserians. This was the idea that the
poetry of these older writers belonged to an order of art
distinct from the classical order to which modern poetry
sought to conform. To compare the ancient epics of Homer
and Virgil with *The Faerie Queene,* John Hughes wrote
in 1715, was as unfair as to compare the "natural grandeur
and simplicity" of Roman architecture with the mixed
"beauty and barbarism" of a Gothic building. Hughes'
language nonetheless implies a superiority in the classical mode that is still apparent a decade later in Pope's
application of this architectural analogy to Shakespeare.
We ought to look upon his works, Pope thought,

> in comparison of those that are more finished and reg-
> ular, as upon an ancient majestic piece of Gothic archi-
> tecture compared with a neat modern building: the
> latter is more elegant and glaring, but the former is
> more strong and more solemn. . . . It has much the
> greater variety, and much the nobler apartments, though
> we are often conducted to them by dark, odd, and un-
> couth passages. Nor does the whole fail to strike us with
> greater reverence, though many of the parts are child-
> ish, ill-placed, and unequal to its grandeur.

Whatever the metaphor employed, by now we recognize
the characteristic mixture of admiration and disapproval. It reappears in two other analogies found in
Johnson's *Preface* among other places, those of the garden
versus forest and the jewel box versus mine. As Johnson

renders them, the "points" of the two analogies are nicely correspondent to their respective objects:

> The work of a correct and regular writer is a garden accurately formed and diligently planted, varied with shades, and scented with flowers; the composition of *Shakespeare* is a forest, in which oaks extend their branches, and pines tower in the air, interspersed sometimes with weeds and brambles, and sometimes giving shelter to myrtles and to roses; filling the eye with awful pomp, and gratifying the mind with endless diversity. Other poets display cabinets of precious rarities, minutely finished, wrought into shape, and polished unto brightness. *Shakespeare* opens a mine which contains gold and diamonds in unexhaustible plenty, though clouded by incrustations, debased by impurities, and mingled with a mass of meaner minerals.

Johnson's *Preface* was written just forty years after Pope's, and it evinces a somewhat greater enthusiasm for Shakespeare. Yet although he preferred Shakespeare's inexhaustible mine to the jewel cabinet of Addison's *Cato* (mention of which immediately evoked the comparison), Johnson still saw impurities debasing the gold and brambles cluttering the forest of noble trees. He goes beyond Pope chiefly in recognizing the unparalleled range and variety of Shakespeare's creativity, which could produce myrtles and roses as well as oaks and pines.

But Shakespeare's conquest of the hearts and minds of eighteenth-century Britons was completed only with a fundamental shift of standards that had actually begun several years before Dr. Johnson wrote the words just quoted. Halting and sometimes retrogressive, this process cannot be neatly charted step-by-step in the work of any critic or group of critics. One can however discern a rough overall development from the admission of a Gothic order, inferior, but different and therefore not subject to classical criteria. Imperceptibly, this Gothic order becomes an *equal* alternative, a step that implies historical relativism in judgment. When Pope refuses to try Shake-

speare by Aristotelian laws we are in the first stage of the
process; the second comes when critics begin to assert that
other laws may be as valid as Aristotle's. In the final step,
taken mainly by the Warton brothers and Hurd, critics
look upon Augustan correctness as actually inferior to
sentiment, sublimity, and passion, qualities they discovered—somewhat indiscriminately—in Macpherson's
Ossian, in Spenser and in Milton, in the Old Testament,
and, supremely, in Shakespeare's plays.

Though this new critical dispensation cannot, with
any decent respect for the evidence, be called romanticism,
it certainly removed barriers to the literary revolution
properly of that name. And certainly it is accompanied
by the gradual change of the word romantic from a pejorative term to one of the highest approval. For Rymer
"romantic" had meant something close to "mad," the
opposite of rational and natural. But Joseph Warton expressed his admiration for the "Lo, the poor Indian"
passage in Pope's *Essay on Man* by calling it "beautifully
romantic," as his brother Thomas had epitomized his
sympathetic analysis of Spenser in *Observations on the
Faerie Queene* by labeling him "in short, a romantic poet."

According to the standard of literary excellence which
these men were now recommending, the other kind of
poetry, the "correct" poetry most perfectly realized by
Pope, was something less than *true* poetry. In the *Essay
on Pope* Joseph Warton relegated the most celebrated
poet of the age to a secondary rank on the grounds that
the kinds in which he excelled, the satiric and didactic,
were "not of the most poetic species of poetry." We have
noted the neoclassical antipathy to allegory. By Thomas
Warton's account, Spenser's great allegorical poem fell
into neglect when an insipid taste for poetry of correctness and "delicacy of sentiment" replaced that for poetry
of "imagination" and "sublimity of description." Readers
had come to value conceits and epigrams above the
"majestic imagery" and the "daring strokes of great conception" which, exemplified in Shakespeare and Milton,

they dismissed as "bombast and insipidity." The phrases in quotation marks are Warton's, but most of them became slogans and watchwords of a long and finally triumphant campaign against the Augustan aesthetic.

Even if this campaign had the fortunate effect of opening readers' eyes to beauties in Shakespeare which they had either missed entirely or mistaken for blemishes, it may be questioned whether as a total poetics it represented an improvement. Granted, it was attended by welcome practical consequences besides those that belong to Shakespeare criticism, such as an awakening interest in Milton's minor poems, which were edited by Thomas Warton in 1785. On the other hand poetic theory is dubiously served by such counsel-darkening concepts as Joseph Warton's poetic and not so poetic poetry, or so question-begging a statement of Thomas Warton that *The Faerie Queene* engages "the feelings of the heart, rather than the cold approbation of the head." Metaphors of this kind must of course never be pressed too hard, but Warton's more skeptical readers would certainly have been justified in asking whether poetic rapture had ever been thought to be exclusively a matter of the intellect, or why, even so, it must be cold. The nameless graces by which Spenser captivates his readers, Warton says, are owing to the "faculties of creative imagination" having been "unrestrained by those of deliberate judgment . . . ." The same thing was repeatedly said of Shakespeare, the poet of nature who lacked judgment (art), until the common image of the man of Stratford was of one who had performed poetic miracles without knowing what he was doing. A great part of Coleridge's later critical labors went into a brilliant refutation of this untenable divorce between genius and intelligence. Shakespeare's judgment, Coleridge had to demonstrate, was in fact equal to his genius.

Some allowance can be made for the critical extravagance of Thomas Warton, who when he wrote his *Observations* was a young man assaulting what he con-

sidered, and rightly considered, to be the ramparts of
entrenched prejudice. One notes the more judicious tone
of a later statement, from his *History of English Poetry*,
in which he ascribes Shakespeare's superiority in part to
his having written in a time favorable to "original and true
poetry," genius then being guided but not governed by
judgment. And to other aspects of the new critical school
some positive credit must be given for making possible a
more informed reading of Shakespeare. This school was
concerned with more than overt judgment, the ticking
off of beauties and faults. Whereas Pope and his fellows
had sneered at the so-called pedantries of Lewis Theobald's study of Shakespeare's text, Thomas Warton
showed in a Postscript to the *Observations* how Theobald
had been able to explain a phrase in *Troilus and Cressida*,
which Pope had wrongly guessed at, by reference to an
old history of Troy known in Elizabethan times. Some attention to what Pope dismissed as "all such reading as
was never read" was thus shown to be useful to a full appreciation of Shakespeare and all other such reading as
would always be read. Gone was the attitude that had
derided the historical philology of a Richard Bentley as
a dull and useless form of antiquarianism. In the second
volume of his critique of Pope, Thomas' brother Joseph
made a point of hailing the "victory over a whole army
of wits" Bentley had gained by his *Dissertation on the
Letters of Phalaris* (1697).

This is not to imply that a great deal was accomplished
in this kind of elucidative research. The significant difference between earlier criticism and works like Hurd's
Letters on Chivalry and Romance (1762) or Warton's
History of English Poetry is not so much the historical
method as the historical *sense*: the awareness of past conditions and the willingness to treat them with tolerance.
For it was this historical sense that engendered a less
unquestioning attitude toward current literary fashions
and critical canons. Since these changed with time, the
critic now often substituted explanation for judgment

and, in judgment itself, induction for prescription. This did not mean lawlessness. It did mean that dogmatic and codified rules had at last to give way completely to broad principles tentatively formulated and constantly re-examined. At the same time literary texts began to be employed as historical documents. Ancient song and poetry, Hugh Blair observed in his *Critical Dissertation on Ossian* (1763), are valuable for what they reveal to us of the manners, notions, feelings, pleasures, and customs of ancient peoples. The task Warton set himself in his *History* was not only to chronicle the development of English poetry from its crude origins to its perfection, but also "to faithfully record the features of the time, and preserve the picturesque representations of manners," as he announced in the preface. In this respect past writers, Shakespeare among them, now took on an added interest as mirrors of bygone times.

Important as these new approaches to literary study were in other respects, it is doubtful whether they yielded an estimate of Shakespeare's achievement more just, from a modern point of view, than that rendered by Dr. Johnson. In place of various prepossessions that had tended to warp literary evaluation in earlier decades, it substituted others that seem equally biased in the perspective of two centuries. One such is the primitivism that arose to reverse the Augustan notion that literary excellence came with polished manners and cultural refinement. Even while common opinion still held that Shakespeare had been handicapped by the rudeness of his age, Thomas Blackwell had been led by his study of the Homeric poems to suggest that a highly civilized society could not supply subjects for poetry. Now Blair was claiming that conditions prevailing in so-called barbarous times favored the very spirit of poetry. Anticipating Wordsworth's views, he argued further that the strong feelings inspired by the grand simplicity of nature gave the very language of primitive men "a poetical turn." As the offspring of the imagination rather than the under-

standing, poetry was thought to be "most glowing and
animated in the first stages of society." Several literary
events of the eighteenth century lent credence to the myth
of the primitive: Macpherson's Ossianic poems, believed
by many to have been of ancient composition; the appearance of Thomas Percy's *Reliques of Ancient English
Poetry* (1765); and, most dramatic of all, the "wood-notes
wild" of "our rustic bard" Robert Burns, "this heaven-
taught plowman," to borrow the revealing epithets of
Henry Mackenzie's pioneer review of the Scottish bard's
poems for *The Lounger* in 1786. In a critical atmosphere
permeated by the belief that imaginative creation sorted ill
with social refinement, it was inevitable that the alleged
rudeness of Elizabethan times once used to explain
Shakespeare's failings should be invoked in warrant of
his poetic power.

Closely allied to the primitivistic Shakespeare, a kind
of English Homer, was the Gothic Shakespeare. A foot-
note in the first volume of Warton's *Essay on Pope* attacks the false delicacy of French literary taste that ridi-
cules the *Odyssey*. The same critics who are nauseated
at the description of Eumaeus' cottage and at Nausicaä's
"ill-breeding," Warton writes, cannot abide the "terrible
graces of our irregular Shakespeare," whose *"Gothic
charms"* make a more powerful appeal to the imagination
than classical elegance. So far, fair enough. Unsatisfied
with such reasonable rhetoric, however, the critic then
asks whether any reader is not more affected by the
images of the huge black-plumed helmet and the gi-
gantic arm at the top of the staircase that appear in
Horace Walpole's *Castle of Otranto* than by anything
depicted in Ovid. The thesis that Shakespeare's genius
might have been half stifled had he been born in the Age
of Reason is one still plausibly entertained. But modern
readers are likely to find the limitations of Dr. Johnson's
evaluation of Shakespeare far less offensive than a taste
that could register the same kind of emotive response
to the plays as to the more lurid inventions of the Gothic

novelists. If in this regard one wonders what has become of the norm of *vraisemblance,* he has only to turn to another proponent of Gothicism, Richard Hurd, for the answer. The purpose of poetry, Hurd declared in his tract *On the Idea of Universal Poetry* (1766), is to go beyond nature and appeal "to our wildest fancy, rather than to our cooler sense." Other aspects of the Gothic way are more responsible. Most valuable is the distinction Hurd drew in the *Letters on Chivalry and Romance* between Gothic unity and the classical unity of a single action. Gothic unity is rather a unity of design produced by multiple actions related by their contribution to a common purpose. Hurd is thinking immediately of *The Faerie Queene* but the conception is equally appropriate to the structure of a Shakespeare play.

With the new generation of poets the taste for Shakespeare's poetry preceded the critical defenses offered to justify it. In a letter to Richard West written in 1742 Thomas Gray added Shakespeare's language, long deplored by those who admired him for other things, to the list of beauties which set him above "your Addisons and your Rowes." Two years later Joseph Warton's poem entitled *The Enthusiast: or, the Lover of Nature* asked,

> *What are the lays of artful Addison,*
> *Coldly correct, to* Shakespeare's *Warblings wild?*

But the main theme of eighteenth-century Shakespeare criticism is character analysis. From the time of Nicholas Rowe's Preface to *The Works* (1709) until the end of the century and beyond, nothing in Shakespeare was more admired than his unrivaled characterization. Preoccupation with this theme is apparent from the titles of the most noteworthy critiques: Thomas Whately's *Remarks on Some of the Characters of Shakespeare* (ca. 1770); William Richardson's *Philosophical Analysis and Illustration of Some of Shakespeare's Remarkable Characters* (1774); Maurice Morgann's *Essay on the Dramatic Character of Falstaff* (1777). One of the best known books on Shakespeare written in the next century, William Hazlitt's *Characters of Shakespear's Plays* (1817), has a rich neoclassical ancestry, a fact the author acknowledged when he opened his Preface by quoting Pope's enthusiastic praise of the lifelike and original beings that people Shakespeare's scenes. But there were other developments pointing to a more distant future. In 1753 Charlotte Lennox made a collection of the plays' sources in her *Shakespear Illustrated*. And the studies of Shakespeare's imagery undertaken in our time by Caroline Spurgeon, Edward Armstrong, Wolfgang Clemen, and others were adumbrated in Walter Whiter's *Specimen of a Commentary on Shakespeare* (1794), though less closely than some commentators have implied. Like the method employed by Miss Spurgeon, Whiter's "new principle of criticism" was to examine Shakespeare's language in order to "discover the objects which excited his passions," in what amounts to an associational imagistic study. But his most rewarding contribution is an explication of the poet's meaning by reference to the physical stage of his day and to popular paintings, tapestries, and pageants.

An unfortunate aspect of the Romantics' idolatry of Shakespeare was their disparagement of Dr. Johnson's appraisal of him. Having quoted Pope's Preface with approval, and with only passing reference to two other English Shakespearians of the previous age, Hazlitt then transcribes several pages from Schlegel's dramatic lectures, on the excuse that the divine poet's countrymen, including Johnson, had done him less than justice. Where Shakespeare is the object Hazlitt will brook no moderation of tribute, "for our admiration cannot easily surpass his genius." As for Dr. Johnson, "he was neither a poet nor a judge of poetry," thinks Hazlitt, and therefore totally unqualified to judge Shakespeare. The famous *Preface to Shakespeare*

> looks like a laborious attempt to bury the characteristic merits of his author under a load of cumbrous phrase-

ology, and to weigh his excellences and defects in equal scales, stuffed full of "swelling figures and sonorous epithets." Nor could it be otherwise; Dr. Johnson's general powers of reasoning overlaid his critical sensibility.

Thus Hazlitt, who was a good critic, in 1817; and thus, more or less, other critics good and not so good for a century thereafter. Since we no longer accept their estimate, we have only to suppose that the nineteenth century set itself a critical task to which the legacy of Johnson's commentary was unavailing and thus had to be swept aside. It may be for the reason that his angle of vision is more congenial to the less visionary era in which we have been living that another good critic, who was also a great poet, could render a verdict so opposed to Hazlitt's. In a brief survey of Shakespeare criticism from Dryden to Coleridge, T. S. Eliot, after quoting an entire paragraph from Johnson's *Preface*, was moved to express himself with an enthusiastic emphasis rare in his prose:

> What a valedictory and obituary for any man to receive! My point is that if you assume that the classical criticism of England was grudging in its praise of Shakespeare, I say that no poet could ask more of posterity than to be greatly honoured by the great; and Johnson's words about Shakespeare are great honour.[3]

It is precisely because a dispassionate reader today is likely to think Eliot nearer the mark than Hazlitt that we need to guard against honoring the *Preface* for the wrong reasons. A sound assessment might well take off from the frank concession of another modern student of Johnson, D. Nichol Smith, that there is little new in Johnson's *Preface* except what he says about his editorial labors.[4] Nichol Smith's observation holds for the celebrated refutation of the dramatic unities, for example. Its main value at the time could only have been to lend Johnson's great personal authority to similar pleas for dramatic liberty that had been voiced by others, a tactic justified by the fact that some of his countrymen—and most of Voltaire's

—were still damning Shakespeare's plays by these irrelevant standards.

Even so, there is no reason to claim originality for Johnson's arguments nor for that matter to enter any wholesale certification of their validity. Against the unity of time he argues, soundly enough, that time is, "of all modes of existence, most obsequious to the imagination . . . ." This point however was an old one, having been made as early as the time of the quarrel over Corneille's *Le Cid* in a *Traité de la disposition du poème dramatique,* whose anonymous author argued that the stage setting was addressed to the audience's imagination, which is docile and follows wherever led.[5] Moreover, Johnson's appeal to the imagination is curiously equivocal. He seems to deny it a similar agency in regard to unity of place. Here he can conceive no state of momentary illusion, no "willing suspension of disbelief," between the sheer delusion of believing the stage to be the promontory of Actium and the sober knowledge that it is in fact only a stage in London.

If the reference to Coleridge's overworked phrase defining poetic faith seems unfair, we can turn back to a solution of the problem suggested by Dryden in the *Defence of an Essay.* The strict advocates of the unities, Dryden noticed, failed to distinguish between *real* time and place and *imaginary* time and place. To the argument that a smaller time cannot contain a greater, he replied "that it may represent it; as in a glass or mirror of half-a-yard diameter, a whole room and many persons in it may be seen at once . . . ." In like fashion, the imagination can leap from place to place. The imagination, Dryden perceived, in a near anticipation of Coleridge, is not divorced from the reason, but "in the belief of fiction" it "suffers itself to be so hood-winked, that it may better enjoy the pleasures of fiction . . . ." And certainly it is permissible to wonder how these pleasures could be enjoyed by Dr. Johnson's clear-eyed spectators, for whom the dramatic fable is never, "for a single moment," credible, and who "are always in their senses, and know, from the first act to the last, that the stage is only a stage, and that the players are only players."

The perception that everything depended on the auditors' *not* being in such a state of constant awareness was not Dryden's alone. The author of the *Remarks on the Tragedy of Hamlet* saw clearly enough the dramatic necessity of a "delusion of our imagination" which, though never at odds with reason, allows us to believe the stage to be Denmark and Wilks to be Hamlet. Just three years before Johnson published the *Preface,* Lord Kames had pointed out in the *Elements of Criticism* that although a theater audience may be conscious of deception, such consciousness is "a work of reflection" which is suspended most of the time.[6] And a reviewer of Johnson writing in *The Monthly Review* put it even more succinctly:

> We do not presume to say that the spectators are not always in their senses; or that they do not know (if the question were put to them) that the stage is only a stage and the players only players. But we will venture to say, they are so intent on the scene, as to be absent with regard to every thing else.[7]

If, despite its limitations, Johnson's *Preface* is the finest example of neoclassical Shakespeare criticism, as prevailing current opinion holds, the reason is apparent with every rereading. Compared with other contemporary estimates of the great dramatist, it contains less of what belongs to the attitudes peculiar to a single time and long since evaporated, and proportionately more that modern sensibility can comfortably accept and modern experience confirm. With no great difficulty we can understand how and why Warton's Shakespeare, the Shakespeare of "terrible graces" and "Gothic charms" exercised a momentary appeal. But this is not *our* Shakespeare. What Johnson prized was a Shakespeare whose characters were

> not modified by the customs of particular places, unpractised by the rest of the world; by the peculiarities of

studies or professions, which can operate but upon small numbers; or by the accidents of transient fashions or temporary opinions; they are the genuine progeny of common humanity, such as the world will always supply, and observation will always find.

Since after the lapse of two centuries the creatures of Shakespeare's feigning still impress readers in every country and culture above all for their psychological truth, we are forced to conclude that Johnson's emphasis was right. And not only here. For us too, "Shakespeare approximates the remote, and familiarizes the wonderful"; and it is as true now as in 1765 that he is "more agreeable to the ears of the present age than any other authour equally remote," and so deserves to be studied as a master of the English tongue.

In all he says of Shakespeare the limitations of Johnson's personal taste and literary convictions show themselves mostly in peripheral considerations. In his insight into what sets the greatest of English poets apart from all others, he easily ranks first among the critics of his time.

Notes

Foreword

1. T. S. Eliot, "William Blake," *Selected Essays* (New York, 1950), p. 279, quoted by permission of the publishers, Harcourt, Brace & World, Inc.

Chapter I

1. René Bray, *La Formation de la doctrine classique en France* (Paris, 1961), p. 263.
2. Figured stanzas had been sympathetically discussed in George Puttenham's *The Arte of English Poesie* (1589), but Montaigne condemned the practice in his *Essays*, made available to English readers in John Florio's translation of 1603.
3. Alexandre Maurocordato, *La Critique classique en Angleterre de la Restauration à la mort de Joseph Addison* (Paris, 1964), pp. 30–31.
4. From "Loveliest of Trees" from "A Shropshire Lad"—Authorized Edition—from *The Collected Poems of A.E. Housman*. Copyright 1939, 1940, © 1959 by Holt, Rinehart and Winston, Inc., and The Society of Authors as the literary representative of the Estate of the late A.E. Housman, and Messrs. Jonathan Cape Ltd.

Chapter II

1. Pierre Moreau, *La Critique littéraire en France* (Paris, 1960), p. 79.
2. Samuel H. Monk, *The Sublime: A Study of Critical Theories in XVIII-Century England* (Ann Arbor, 1960), p. 56.
3. It is in specific relation to Hurd's *Letters* that John Butt has

called attention to neoclassicism's power of "adapting itself
to new forms and conditions without changing its essentially
'regular' nature" (*The Augustan Age* [New York, 1966], p.
45).

4. See for example R. F. Jones' "Science and Criticism in the
Neo-Classical Age of English Literature," *Journal of the History of Ideas*, I (1940), 381–412.

5. Monroe C. Beardsley, *Aesthetics from Classical Greece to
the Present: A Short History* (New York, 1966), p. 205.

Chapter III

1. René Bray, *La Formation de la doctrine classique en France*
(Paris, 1961), p. 314.

2. See Cecil V. Deane, *Dramatic Theory and the Rhymed
Heroic Play* (London, 1931), esp. Chapter 5; also Arthur C.
Kirsch, *Dryden's Heroic Dramas* (Princeton, 1965), p. 127.

3. Northrop Frye, *Anatomy of Criticism* (Princeton, 1957), p.
39.

4. Moody E. Prior, "Tragedy and the Heroic Play," in *Dryden:
A Collection of Critical Essays,* ed. Bernard N. Schilling
(Englewood Cliffs, N.J., 1963), p. 100.

Chapter IV

1. René Bray, *La Formation de la doctrine classique en France*
(Paris, 1961), pp. 190, 163.

2. Alexandre Maurocordato, *La Critique classique en Angleterre* . . . (Paris, 1964), p. 177.

3. Quoted from *Four Quartets* (New York, 1943), p. 17, by
permission of the publishers, Harcourt, Brace & World, Inc.

4. Northrop Frye, *Fables of Identity: Studies in Poetic Mythology* (New York, 1963), pp. 42, 47.

5. Northrop Frye, *Anatomy of Criticism* (Princeton, 1957), pp.
97–98. Like many other insights of this perceptive critic, this
one does not depend for its force on the intricate mythopoeic
critical system which Frye has sought to elucidate in his
Anatomy and elsewhere, and which, as a system, is obviously
anything but "neoclassical."

6. *Ibid.*, p. 101.

7. Paul Fussell, Jr., *Poetic Meter and Poetic Form* (New York,
1965).

8. John Crowe Ransom, "Poetry: A Note on Ontology," in *The
World's Body* (Port Washington, N.Y., 1964), p. 114.

Chapter V

1. René Wellek, *A History of Modern Criticism 1750–1950* (New Haven, 1955), Vol. I (*The Later Eighteenth Century*), p. 79.

2. George Saintsbury, *A History of Criticism and Literary Taste in Europe* (Edinburgh, 1900–1904), Vol. II, p. 484.

3. J. W. H. Atkins, *English Literary Criticism: 17th and 18th Centuries* (London, 1951), p. 275.

4. Walter Jackson Bate, *The Achievement of Samuel Johnson* (New York, 1955), p. 194.

5. T. S. Eliot, "Johnson as Critic and Poet," in *On Poetry and Poets* (New York, 1957), p. 210.

6. F. R. Leavis, "Johnson and Augustanism," in *The Common Pursuit* (London, 1952), p. 111.

7. Bate, *The Achievement of Samuel Johnson*, p. 219.

8. William K. Wimsatt, Jr., *The Prose Style of Samuel Johnson* (New Haven, 1963), pp. 55–56, quoted by permission of the publisher, Yale University Press.

9. Allen Tate, "Johnson on the Metaphysical Poets," in *Samuel Johnson: A Collection of Critical Essays,* ed. Donald J. Greene (Englewood Cliffs, N.J., 1965), pp. 98–99.

10. See William R. Keast, "Johnson's Criticism of the Metaphysical Poets," *ELH*, XVII (1950), 59–70.

Chapter VI

1. T. S. Eliot, "Shakespearian Criticism: I. From Dryden to Coleridge," in *A Companion to Shakespeare Studies,* ed. Harley Granville-Barker and G. B. Harrison (New York, 1934), p. 290.

2. See John Butt, *Pope's Taste in Shakespeare,* Shakespeare Association Paper no. 20 (London, 1936), pp. 9, 17.

3. Eliot, "Shakespearian Criticism: I. From Dryden to Coleridge," p. 294.

4. D. Nichol Smith, "Introduction" to *Shakespeare Criticism: A Selection, 1623–1840* (London, 1961), p. xii.

5. René Bray, *La Formation de la doctrine classique* (Paris, 1961), p. 278.

6. Quoted in Clarence C. Green, *The Neo-Classic Theory of Tragedy* (Cambridge, Mass., 1934), p. 208.

7. *Ibid.,* p. 213.

For Further Reading

A. Anthologies

Durham, Willard H., ed. *Critical Essays of the Eighteenth Century 1700–1725.* New Haven, 1915.

Elledge, Scott, ed. *Eighteenth-Century Critical Essays.* 2 vols. Ithaca, N.Y., 1961.

Jones, Edmund D., ed. *English Critical Essays (Sixteenth, Seventeenth, and Eighteenth Centuries).* London, 1922.

Needham, H. A., ed. *Taste and Criticism in the Eighteenth Century.* London, 1952.

Smith, D. Nichol, ed. *Eighteenth-Century Essays on Shakespeare.* Glasgow, 1903.

Spingarn, J. E., ed. *Critical Essays of the Seventeenth Century.* 3 vols. Bloomington, Ind., 1957.

B. Some Modern Editions

Brown, Joseph Epes. *The Critical Opinions of Samuel Johnson.* Princeton, 1926.

Goldgar, Bertrand A., ed. *Literary Criticism of Alexander Pope.* Lincoln, Neb., 1965.

Hill, G. B., ed. *Lives of the English Poets by Samuel Johnson, Ll.D.* 3 vols. Oxford, 1905.

Hooker, Edward Niles, ed. *The Critical Works of John Dennis.* 2 vols. Baltimore, 1939, 1943.

Ker, W. P., ed. *The Essays of John Dryden.* 2 vols. Oxford, 1900.

Raleigh, Walter, ed. *Johnson on Shakespeare.* London, 1908.

Sir Joshua Reynolds, *Discourses on Art,* ed. Robert R. Wark. San Marino, Calif., 1959.

Watson, George, ed. *John Dryden: Of Dramatic Poesy and Other*

Critical Essays. 2 vols. New York, 1962 (Everyman's Library).

Zimansky, Curt A., ed. *The Critical Works of Thomas Rymer.* New Haven, 1956.

C. Commentary

Atkins, J. W. H. *English Literary Criticism: 17th and 18th Centuries.* London, 1951.

Babcock, Robert Witbeck. *The Genesis of Shakespeare Idolatry 1766–1799.* Chapel Hill, 1931.

Bate, Walter Jackson. *The Achievement of Samuel Johnson.* New York, 1955.

———. *From Classic to Romantic.* Cambridge, Mass., 1946.

Bosker, A. *Literary Criticism in the Age of Johnson,* second edition, revised. New York, 1953.

Bray, René. *La Formation de la doctrine classique en France.* Paris, 1927.

Bredvold, Louis I. *The Intellectual Milieu of John Dryden.* Ann Arbor, 1934.

Clark, A. F. B. *Boileau and the French Classical Critics in England (1660–1700).* Paris, 1925.

Crane, R. S. "English Neoclassical Criticism: An Outline Sketch," in *Critics and Criticism.* Chicago, 1952.

Elioseff, Lee Andrew. *The Cultural Milieu of Addison's Literary Criticism.* Austin, Tex., 1963.

Eliot, T. S. *John Dryden.* New York, 1932.

———. "The Age of Dryden," in *The Use of Poetry and the Use of Criticism.* Cambridge, Mass., 1933.

Gallaway, Francis. *Reason, Rule, and Revolt in English Classicism.* New York, 1940.

Green, Clarence C. *The Neo-Classic Theory of Tragedy in England During the Eighteenth Century.* Cambridge, Mass., 1934.

Hagstrum, Jean. *Samuel Johnson's Literary Criticism.* Minneapolis, 1952.

———. *The Sister Arts.* Chicago, 1958.

Keast, W. R. "The Theoretical Foundations of Johnson's Criticism," in *Critics and Criticism,* ed. R. S. Crane. Chicago, 1952.

Krutch, Joseph Wood. *Samuel Johnson.* New York, 1944.

Leavis, F. R. "Johnson and Augustanism," in *The Common Pursuit.* London, 1952.

Maurocordato, Alexandre. *La Critique classique en Angleterre de la Restauration à la mort de Joseph Addison.* Paris, 1964.

Monk, Samuel H. *The Sublime: A Study of Critical Theories in XVIII-Century England.* New York, 1935.

Tate, Allen. "Johnson on the Metaphysical Poets," in *Samuel Johnson: A Collection of Critical Essays,* ed. Donald J. Greene. Englewood Cliffs, N.J., 1965.

Warren, Austin. *Alexander Pope as Critic and Humanist.* Princeton, 1929.

Wellek, René. "Neoclassicism and the New Trends of the Time" and "Dr. Johnson," in *A History of Modern Criticism 1750–1950.* 5 vols. I (*The Later Eighteenth Century*). New Haven, 1955.

———. *The Rise of English Literary History.* Chapel Hill, 1941.

Willey, Basil. *The Eighteenth Century Background.* London, 1940.

Wimsatt, William K., Jr., and Cleanth Brooks. *Literary Criticism: A Short History.* New York, 1957 (pp. 174–336).

Index